Stories from Child & Adol Psychotherapy

In *Stories from Child & Adolescent Psychotherapy* author Henry Kronengold explores the unpredictable world of child and adolescent psychotherapy through a series of engaging and innovative clinical vignettes. The ups, downs, and dilemmas of therapeutic work are considered in each realistic narrative as readers are offered a unique view of what happens between the therapist and child, as well as the therapist's own process during the therapy. This captivating new resource is intended to spark a conversation within the reader, regardless of professional experience or orientation, regarding which therapeutic factors are ultimately most helpful to children and adolescents.

Henry Kronengold, PhD, maintains a private practice in New York City. He is a clinical supervisor at the Clinical Psychology Program at the City University of New York.

Stories from Child & Adolescent Psychotherapy

A Curious Space

Henry Kronengold

Routledge
Taylor & Francis Group

NEW YORK AND LONDON

First published 2017
by Routledge
711 Third Avenue, New York, NY 10017

and by Routledge
2 Park Square, Milton Park, Abingdon, Oxon, OX14 4RN

Routledge is an imprint of the Taylor & Francis Group, an informa business

© 2017 Taylor & Francis

Library of Congress Cataloging-in-Publication Data
Names: Kronengold, Henry, author.
Title: Stories from child & adolescent psychotherapy: a curious space /
by Henry Kronengold. Other titles: Stories from child and adolescent psychotherapy
Description: New York, NY: Routledge, 2016.
Includes bibliographical references and index.
Identifiers: LCCN 2016014743 | ISBN 9781138912861 (hbk: alk. paper) |
ISBN 9781138912878 (pbk: alk. paper) | ISBN 9781315691732 (ebk)
Subjects: | MESH: Mental Disorders—therapy | Psychotherapy—methods |
Child | Adolescent
Classification: LCC RC480.5 NLM WS 350 DDC 616.89/14—dc23
LC record available at https://lccn.loc.gov/2016014743

ISBN: 978-1-138-91286-1 (hbk)
ISBN: 978-1-138-91287-8 (pbk)
ISBN: 978-1-315-69173-2 (ebk)

Typeset in Sabon
by codeMantra

Dedicated with love and gratitude to Jill, Max, and Nina

Contents

Acknowledgments

I would like to express my appreciation to numerous colleagues, friends, and family members who have supported me during the process of writing this book. First and foremost, I would like to thank Jill Putterman, my wife and my colleague, for all of her help with this book. Jill helped with extensive comments, support, and an overall enthusiasm for this project, which has proved beyond invaluable during the writing of this book.

A number of colleagues and friends have read and commented on different cases in this book. I want to thank David Crenshaw and Ana Sutton, whose feedback and encouragement have been so critical to me since they read the first of these case studies some years ago. My introduction to Ana, via David, led me to the Wroxton International Play Therapy Study Group, a special collection of therapists from around the world led by Charlie Schaefer. My experiences in Wroxton have in many ways inspired and cultivated my continued writing. I would particularly like to thank David Le Vay, Eileen Prendiville, Majella Ryan, John Seymour, Evangeline Munns, and Claudio Mochi for their feedback on different sections of this book. I would like to thank the rest of my fellow Wroxtonites for their friendship, inspiration, curiosity, and of course, playfulness.

Closer to home, I have been helped by a number of very talented and thoughtful individuals who have read and offered feedback on different chapters of this book or inspired me with our conversations. I am most grateful and offer my heartfelt thanks to Ben Harris, John Mathews, Carol Eagle, Chris Bonovitz, Leslie Sharpe, Joe Reynoso, Jasmine Ueng-Mchale, Rise Van Fleet, Peter Carnochan, Ann Flick, Kenneth Barish, Leslie Epstein-Pearson, Lois Carey, Tzachi Slonim, Frumi Strohli, and Ben Lapkin.

I have also had the pleasure of feedback and communication with colleagues in different countries who have generously given of their time to read and consider these case studies and engage in a clinical dialogue regardless of the physical distance. I would like to thank Gunnar Carlberg from Sweden and Peter Blake from Australia, who have been generous to consider and discuss the many relevant clinical and theoretical factors related to working with children as they arise in these case studies. I would also like to thank Antonino Ferro and Roberto Basile, from Italy, for their time and feedback on the early chapters.

Stories from Child & Adolescent Psychotherapy: A Curious Space would not have happened without the support of my editor, Chris Teja, who I thank for his belief and support for this project. Finally, I will return to my family for their encouragement during the writing of this book. These cases were written over several years, with a certain waxing and waning of my enthusiasm for writing over that time. Jill, Max, Nina, and the rest of my family have helped keep me going as this project came to its completion and I am enormously grateful for all of your support.

A Note on Confidentiality

This book is a collection of therapeutic narratives. My writing about each child is part of my own wondering about psychotherapy and I am hopeful that the stories in this book add to the discussion of how we help children and adolescents. My writing also involves publishing a set of experiences and exchanges that occur in the privacy of the therapy room. I have taken a number of steps to maintain the confidentiality of the individuals in this book. All names used in this book are fictitious. I have provided as little personal and family history as possible in order to protect the privacy of the children and families discussed. In addition, a number of changes have been made with respect to family or personal history in order to protect confidentiality while not changing the essence of the clinical material. It is my sincerest hope that the privacy of the individuals in this book has been maintained as I have tried to write about each young person and his or her family in a manner that is both humane and respectful.

1   Introduction

A Curious Space

In the middle of a session, many years ago, a ten-year-old boy looked at me as we tossed a ball back and forth. He hesitated for a moment before asking me, "*what are we doing?*" as he wondered how therapy helped him. He surprised me that day with his question, but in truth, he was only echoing what I often ask myself. I see children and teenagers of various ages and challenges and I play and talk with them. I meet with parents, teachers, and anyone else who may prove helpful to a child's development. I'm confident that I can help children and their families. At the same time, I often wonder about what helps in therapy. What actually happens between a therapist and children that allows for progress and healing?

"What are we doing?" This question is central to how I came to write this book. At some point I decided that while I'd continue searching for answers, I'd also embrace the question and its openness about child work. This is a book of case studies, or what I prefer to see as short stories, detailing my work and the therapeutic relationships I developed with six different children and adolescents.

These stories focus on the therapeutic process, and include many of the uncomfortable moments that occur in therapy. The therapy stories I chose to tell are not the ones with the best outcomes, nor are they in truth, the worst. Rather, they are therapies that have left me wondering about the critical factors that are helpful in working with children. Each of these children challenged me to think about crucial aspects of the therapeutic process. To what extent do we follow a child's lead? To what extent do we encourage a child to handle a challenge when it provokes discomfort? At what point do we consider a child's repetitive play or behavior a problem in therapy? Must the therapist have a clear idea of what is happening in a particular therapy in order to help a child? What about the role of banter and humor? Sports? Winning and losing? To what extent does the therapist's own presence play a critical role in the work? How much is therapy co-created between therapist and child? How do we handle endings, being paid, or myriad personal questions headed in our direction?

These are some of the questions that I consider and which I think resonate for most child therapists. Each child is different and while there is a similar style underlying how I worked with these children, I also chose different paths in each of the cases. At times, my approaches may seem contradictory, which speaks to my own belief that rather than following one particular orientation, we need to consider the individual needs of each child and tailor our therapeutic approach appropriately. Of course I have my biases as to what is important in therapy, and I am quite sure they are reflected in these vignettes. Much of my work and training flows from psychoanalytic, humanistic, and developmental traditions, and their emphasis on the importance of play in child development and therapy. That said, I also utilize cognitive, behavioral, family systems, and sensorimotor approaches in my work. My hope is that these cases are sufficiently roomy so that any reader who is curious about therapeutic work with children will find these stories relatable and stimulating.

I freely admit to my focus on the importance of the therapeutic relationship, to the underlying meaning of what happens in a therapy session, and to the spirit of curiosity and adventure that I think are crucial to working with children. There is a sense of fun and playfulness in these sessions, even amidst the most poignant and difficult of moments. There is a wondering about the therapeutic process that stems from the experience and appreciation of the complicated lives and developmental paths of the young people who enter our offices or playrooms. The more I work, the more complexity I find as to what is and isn't helpful to children. It is enticing to read a book or manual that seems to hold all the answers. If only it were that easy.

A quote from Antonino Ferro (1999) comes to mind when thinking about the individuality and complexity of children. He discusses a young girl, Francesca, who drew pictures in his office of a forest, called *the wood*. Ferro talks of looking at Francesca's drawing and holding back from prematurely determining its meaning so that he can come closer to the child's point of view.

> Once I loosen the ties to my theoretical referents, I begin to sense the risk of getting lost. "Weak" models expose us to the fear of thinking and finding ourselves alone in the wood, whereas "strong" models would make us feel safe, but they would allow us to see in the wood only what the models themselves had already prefigured.
>
> *(p. 27)*

I offer Ferro's quote as an introduction to these stories and an invitation to take in and consider the different children whom I will discuss. I invite the reader with me into the therapeutic space. I invite the reader to wonder and to be curious with me. To get a little lost in considering what may happen in a particular therapy. Once we allow ourselves to get lost, we also allow ourselves to jump into a child's world, a central attitude that underlies my attempts to help each of the children in this book. By necessity, we may not always know what we are doing, as jumping into someone else's world necessitates a certain discomfort and suspension of knowledge. The feeling is uncomfortable, and the rush of trying to find one's bearings can lead to much confusion or to a desire to quickly structure the therapy in a way that is predictable and comfortable.

It is critical to genuinely play, to join a child and sometimes get lost, as a co-player, with that child in his or her world. Entering a child's world and seeking to understand a child means that the therapist walks with a sense of purpose and playfulness, but also humility that comes from trying to understand another person and realizing that there is much to learn in the process. This very experience is powerful and therapeutic, whether the therapist engages in the child's world through play, art, talking, or whatever medium the child uses in his or her experience. If the child plays baseball, then the therapist can become a baseball player. If she or he draws, then the therapist may become an artist, and if the child enjoys puppets, then by all means, one can grab a puppet and create characters with the child, developing a shared and imaginative space that drives a treatment. It is also important to note that if a child approaches the world mostly by talking, then one can engage a child verbally in that same sense of discovery.

There are children whose play enters a fantastical world, and such play can be rich and great fun. But the wonder and discovery of play can just as easily be grounded in play that mimics reality, such as a board game, active physical play, or verbal back and forth. To the extent that each child creates his or her world in a different way, it is our job to enter into it, without preconceived notions of what or how that world should be. But, again, not to just follow along, but to jump in, so that like any good playmate or partner, we co-create narratives, develop an engaged relationship, and hold onto affective experiences that help a child move forward developmentally.

I can think of older children who rely on metaphor and younger children who work best with a verbal model of therapy. The difference is how each child experiences and approaches the world. To me, the question is how we consider our therapeutic work in light of a given child's different tendencies, so that we make room for that child's dynamically evolving approach to the world in the space of our therapy room. It is important to consider how this therapeutic space is co-created by two people, the child and the therapist, and that the therapist brings his or her own proclivities and tendencies to the relationship. I happen to enjoy sports, Lego, and in the form of back and forth banter, engage children with humor. Though I enjoy art, I happen to be a truly awful artist. Sadly, this lack of skill can impact my sessions as well. The idea is that each therapist I think needs to consider how she or he can best connect to a child, while being respectful of the child and honest about the therapist's own preferred way of working. It is our connection with a child that underlies so much of what we do in therapy. There is an old tale that has stayed with me since I first heard it long before I started my training as a child therapist. The Hasidic story of the Rooster Prince has much to teach us about working with children who are vulnerable.

Once upon a time a prince lived with his parents in a city in Eastern Europe. Every day the king gave his son tasks and instructions for how to behave. "Be polite to all the elders. Behave in a princely fashion. Speak this way, walk that way."

One day the prince woke at dawn, sat up, and began to crow like a rooster. At first no one paid much attention, but when he took off his clothes and waddled downstairs, still crowing at the top of his lungs, the servants began to laugh. The queen was in the kitchen eating breakfast, and when she saw her son, she gasped. "My dear, go put on some clothes! You're not behaving like a prince!" But the prince ignored her and crouched under the table where he began to peck at the crumbs on the floor, just as a rooster might. The king scowled. "This is hardly princely behavior. We are not amused!"

But no matter what the king and queen said or did, the prince crowed and waddled and pecked and behaved in every way like a rooster, not like a prince. That evening, instead of going to his room, the prince padded out to the barn, and there he spent the night. At dawn he opened his eyes and began to crow, and soon he trundled back into the house to sit beneath the kitchen table and peck at the crumbs on the floor. This went on, day after day.

In despair, the king and queen called upon an assortment of royal doctors who offered pills, spells, rituals, and tried talking sense to him, but the prince crowed in their faces. "What can we do to make our son behave like a prince once again?" the king asked his wise men, but nobody had an answer, and soon word spread of the rooster prince.

One day an old sage came to the city. His face lined with age, his eyes nearly invisible, the sage limped along with the help of his cane. He made his way to the palace and announced, "I assure the king and queen I have the cure for their son." The king pointed to the kitchen where the prince now spent his days under the table, and the sage limped there. The king followed and stood in startled silence as the old sage undressed, climbed under the table, and began to cluck and peck like a chicken. "How can you cure my son of his madness if you are mad as well?" the king cried. But the sage only clucked more loudly and scurried about, pecking for crumbs. The king and queen consulted with each other. "What shall we do?" the queen pleaded. "Now we have two madmen in our home." "We must wait," said the king, though his heart swelled with worry.

The next day the rooster and the chicken, the prince and the sage, pecked away under the table, clucking and crowing, and as they pecked, they began to talk to each other. "I'm a rooster," said the prince. "So you are," the sage said, "and how is your life here in the kitchen?" "Fine indeed," the prince said. "Everyone leaves me alone to enjoy my time. It's a fine life." "I understand," the sage said.

This went on until one day the sage called to the royal seamstress. "Bring me a pair of pants," he said. When the seamstress brought them, the sage began to put them on. The rooster prince stared and cried, "What are you doing? Chickens don't wear pants!" "Who says?" the sage asked. "Why shouldn't I be warm? Why should humans have all the good things?" For the first time the rooster prince noticed the floor was cold and the barn too; the next day, when the sage asked for a shirt, the rooster prince stared and said, "Chickens don't wear shirts." "Why should I shiver just because I'm a chicken?" the sage answered. Once again the rooster prince thought about how cold he felt, and when the sage put on socks and shoes, the rooster prince saw how bruised and tired his own feet were. Shortly thereafter, the prince returned to his station, having given up the life of a rooster.

I will leave the reader to consider the meanings of the Rooster Prince story, just as I trust the reader to consider the meanings of my own stories in this book. For me, this tale speaks to the power of what can happen when one individual allows him or herself to enter into the world of another, and in the process, to both connect to that person and to help that person move to a different place. But there are many ways to look at the story, just as there are many ways to consider our work with children. This book is called a curious space. There is the therapist's curiosity in trying to understand and help a child and in trying to think about what approaches may help a child in a given moment. There is the curiosity of the child, frequently absent early in therapy, which is hopefully sparked in the therapeutic space and whose momentum can be so powerful as a child grows. Then there is the other sense of curiosity, the sense of puzzlement and wonder about what happens in therapy as we try to understand the moments in which a therapist and a particular child meet. It is that sense of curiosity that inspires my work with children and which I hope emerges and is stimulated by the therapy stories in this book. The idea of this book is not so much to answer the question of what we are doing, as much as it is to allow this question to simmer, and stimulate ideas about working with children and adolescents. I hope the reader will accept my invitation and join me in pondering the therapeutic process, at least as it unfolds with six very different young people and one particular therapist.

2   Hey Toy Man

I first meet children when I walk out of my office and greet them in the waiting area. They are usually tentative, wondering who they're about to meet and what they're about to do. Abby was not one of those children.

I walked out of my office and said hello to a tall and lanky six-year-old girl with long brown hair. Ensconced in pink, Abby smiled quickly, gave a brusque hello, and as I looked at the contents of her knapsack spread out on a waiting room chair, seemed to have made herself right at home. I invited Abby into my office and she followed easily. Actually, I followed, as Abby bounced in to begin our first session and immediately starting looking around and exploring. She first looked at a toy castle, then a basket filled with nerf balls, before she noticed the door to my toy closet slightly ajar. Opening it, her eyes widened as she looked through the closet trying to decide what to do first. She searched quickly but methodically through the closet before settling on the contents of a play kitchen, including pots, plates, and all manner of pretend food.

Abby was one of those children who gets tagged as *energetic* or *spirited*. As in her recent Kindergarten teacher's report – "Abby is an energetic and spirited child who loves to be creative and is learning how to follow classroom rules and play with other children," which was a nice way of saying that Abby wasn't listening to her teachers or making any friends. Abby liked to do what she wanted and was otherwise uncooperative. Abby's mother echoed these concerns, telling me how Abby became easily frustrated at small disappointments and was having frequent temper tantrums at home. Adopted as a month-old infant from a small village in Romania, with little known about her biological parents, Abby was now living a comfortable life in Manhattan with her adoptive mother and a ten-year-old sister, who was also adopted. Abby's mother, a successful attorney, was very patient, and as is often the case for a parent, was quite exhausted and just not sure what to do next.

In the early days of our two-year therapy, I felt as if our sessions began before Abby entered my office. I would hear Abby as she sat in the waiting room, talking animatedly to her mother or her babysitter. As soon as I would open the door, she would bounce up, and dive quickly into play, greatly enjoying the different games and materials. In our early sessions, Abby liked to experiment with different items, playing with pretend food, building with blocks, and taking out paper and markers to draw. But most of all, more than any of the toys and games, Abby loved to boss me around, her voice sharpening as she told me what and what not to do.

> Stand over here! Get that box! No! Not the red one! The green one! You set it up the wrong way! How many times do I have to tell you that I don't like that one! Over there already!

While this may sound grating, and at times it was, there was something endearing about the way Abby ordered me around. It helped that Abby seemed to enjoy and invest herself in the sessions, which told me that her controlling behavior was probably going to be important in some way in the stories and characters we would ultimately create. Often, controlling behavior serves to stop a line of questioning or an avenue of play. But in Abby's case, it seemed to be a main character in the play. It also helped that as Abby bossed me around, she did so with a twinkle in her eye, hinting at an underlying motivation that I suspected would prove meaningful. So, I played along, working as a cross between hired help and indentured servant.

(Abby, sitting on the carpet building a house, looks up at me as I approach)
ABBY: You can't sit here. This is my place.
ME: Abby, can I sit over here? (pointing to a spot to her left)
ABBY: No!
ME: How about here? (I point to a spot a little further to the left)
ABBY: That's a little better, but not quite. Move that way! (Abby points imperiously to a spot on the right)
ME: Ok, Ok. Gee, a little touchy. Yes ma'am.
ABBY: Don't call me ma'am (her voice turning chilly at this point)
ME: What should I call you?
ABBY: By my name. (She looks at me as if I couldn't be a bigger fool)
ME: Ok. I think I'm getting it now.
ABBY: No. You're not! (as she turns up her nose and looks away)

Abby also provided me with a special name. To Abby, I was *Toy Man*. As in, "Hey Toy Man." "See you next week Toy Man." Or more commonly, "Stand over here, Toy Man!" "Get that box, Toy Man!" or "Out of my way Toy Man." When we disagreed, Abby would furl her brow, put her hands on her hips, look at me intently, and begin – "Listen Toy Man ..."

I decided to just go with it. I was *Toy Man*. In Abby's case, it got to the point where even her babysitter didn't know my real name, sheepishly calling me *Toy Man* one day when asking me a question about Abby's schedule. I thought about the significance of *Toy Man*. What did it mean? Why wouldn't Abby relate to me by calling me by my real name? Was naming me *Toy Man* a way for Abby to keep a distance from me, just as she kept a distance from the children at school? Maybe *Toy Man* had to do with Abby's history of early loss, as the shift from her biological to her adopted family may have left her wary of bringing in a new person, especially an adult man, as Abby had no father and few adult males in her life. I wondered whether to say anything about it to Abby or attempt to interpret the meaning of this particular moniker. Or should I just let myself be called *Toy Man*, and decipher its meaning as our time together unfolded?

I also began to realize that most of my questions suggested that *Toy Man* was a problem, a way that Abby needed to make me into an imaginary character for some defensive purpose. Maybe my thinking was off base. Looking around my office, I had to admit the name made sense. Maybe it had to do with the fact that for 45 minutes a week, the two of us were entering into a place of pretend, where the typical rules and bounds of reality didn't always apply. Maybe being called *Toy Man* in this situation made perfect sense.

Abby was a most enthusiastic player. She liked to play active ball games and began to experiment with some of my pretend characters and puppets. When she tried to use the pretend toys to develop stories though, she offered clipped details that were difficult to follow. It went like this –

> This is the mommy and the daddy and here are the babies. They are going on a trip together. They're flying on a plane. Mommy picks up the babies and holds them. She tells the babies how much she loves them and puts them down on their seats. They're home now. It's time for lunch.

Abby was just emerging as a storyteller, and her fractured stories, with babies and mommies flying on airplanes, clearly held symbolic meaning. But her play lacked detail and she rarely followed a sequence. Where did the babies come from? Where were they going? What were they doing flying around so much anyway?

Without much success, I tried to clarify and structure the meaning of Abby's stories, asking her questions to elicit more narrative detail. Abby responded by telling me to go pick up the toys, before letting me know I wasn't putting them back the right way. In response, I tried to make sense of her behavior. My interventions consisted of brilliant comments such as, "Whenever I ask you a question, I feel like I'm annoying you," or the even better, "I wonder if there are other people you talk to this way?" Abby would look back at me for a second, wearing a look of such utter disdain. Did I really think she was going to respond to these comments? So I cleaned up and organized puppets, set up building toys, and in general, did Abby's bidding. I realized I faced the risk of indulging Abby, only fueling her tendency to become frustrated and have tantrums. But, when I thought about her play, at once so intriguing yet so confused, and I also considered her behavior, in my office so controlling, yet everywhere else so out of control, I felt compelled to engage with Abby in her world and to help her make sense of whatever she was feeling and trying to say. Maybe then, she could let go a little with me and let go a little less with everyone else.

As we got to know each other, our symbolic play began in earnest, as Abby gave me detailed instructions to use my toy storage boxes, carefully emptied of their contents, to set up a house with two well-guarded doors. Abby resided inside the house with several of my puppets and a baby doll. I was told to stay outside the house, with two of the bear puppets keeping me company. For several weeks, Abby had us play out a scenario where my puppets tried to get into the house but were denied entry. At times, they were teased with promises of treats, only to have the front door rudely slammed shut by a smiling Abby. At this point, the echoes of our relationship interested me, but less so than the story's emerging structure. For the first time, I could easily follow Abby's storylines, and though they were brief, I trusted that more detail would be forthcoming.

Abby next put me in charge of two bear puppets, who were in love and engaged to be married. Their upcoming marriage was thwarted by an old lady living in the neighboring house, who invited in the female bear and turned her into a baby. In her infant state, the bear didn't remember her fiancé at all, and lived in the care of the woman from the house. Meanwhile, her fiancé desperately tried to reach his beloved. He knocked on windows, tried to call her, and pleaded with the old lady for her release. All to no avail, as the old lady ordered him away from her property. Dejected, the fiancé bear slumped off, wandering outside of the house and its environs. Soon, the lady in the house, who was slowly becoming known as the princess, offered the bear some new information.

PRINCESS: You see she is not really your wife.

BEAR: Huh?

PRINCESS: She's not your wife.

BEAR: Then who is she?

PRINCESS: She's your sister (with a gleeful quality to her voice).

BEAR: You turned her into a baby!

PRINCESS: (In a gentle voice explains) That was for her own good. Your wife is someone else. She looks exactly like your wife but she really is your sister. She was switched when you weren't looking.

BEAR: Then where is my beloved wife?

PRINCESS: Umm. You have to find her.

BEAR: But where?

PRINCESS: That's your problem (she said coldly).

BEAR: What do you mean it's my problem; you're the one with all the information (At this point I'm asking in a half-pleading, half-frustrated voice).

PRINCESS: I've done everything I can for you. Now go!

BEAR: This is really confusing.

PRINCESS: Go find her.

BEAR: Can you give me a clue?

PRINCESS: No. I'm sorry. I really can't (as she closes the pretend door to the house).

So the bear went off to find his wife, a bit suspicious of the princess and whether she was being completely honest about the whole sister–wife change story. The bear looked everywhere, but each time he thought he was getting close – a bear sighting, a bracelet, a photograph – he came away empty handed.

As this drama continued to unfold, the princess added a new request, asking me to get her some ice cream at the local ice cream shop. The Princess wasn't content to have just one ice cream cone or cup. Rather, she bought the entire store and had it shipped back to her house. It so happened that the bear wanted some ice cream as well, but the Princess would get to the store just before the bear, who was ready with his order, only to learn that all the ice cream, and at times, even all the utensils and store fixtures, had just been sold. Dejected, he pleaded for just a bit of leftover dessert, but, as Abby the shopkeeper gleefully explained, everything in the store was gone. So, the bear turned around and went off on his way. He had no wife, no clue where to find her, and, to add insult to injury, no dessert either.

Taking a step back, I was thrilled with the development of Abby's story. Our sessions, which had only recently seen the emergence of a cogent plot, had moved to full-blown narratives, with intriguing twists and turns. There was a broken romance, a bride taken and turned into a child, and a forlorn groom searching for his love, all orchestrated by a princess who took equal delight in her own indulgence as in her perceived rival's deprivation. I wondered if we were getting to the root of Abby's difficulties, and wanted to say something about what she might have been feeling inside. But my earlier attempts at connecting Abby's stories to her feelings had only frustrated her, and I also knew that we were very early in this story. So I kept quiet and played.

Abby left the bears and shifted to playing with some of the human figures that belong to the playhouse in my office. She enthusiastically selected families for each of us, including a mother, grandmother, and two children, a boy and a girl, for herself, and a mother, father, grandmother, and a daughter for me. I arranged my characters, not remarking on the differences between our family constellations.

ABBY: (In a cheerful voice) now the families are going on a trip. They have to get to the airport to take a plane.
ME: Where are they going?
ABBY: No one knows (adding a mysterious tone to her voice).
ME: No one? (I ask with my eyebrows raised).
ABBY: Well there is one person who does.
ME: Who?
ABBY: Don't know.
ME: But you just said there is someone who knows where they're going?
ABBY: Yes there is.
ME: Who? (I ask with more frustration in my voice)

ABBY: I told you no one knows. It's a mystery.

ME: OhhhhKayyyy. (I respond, as if in an Abbott & Costello routine) So what happens?

ABBY: Get them ready for the trip.

ME: Come on everyone, get your stuff, your suitcases. Is everyone ready to go? (There's an exchange between the family members who agree they're all set to go). Alright, we're ready.

ABBY: The car is here, everyone climb in. (Everyone is set).

ME: Here we go kids, wherever it is that we're going.

ABBY: We're at the train station now.

ME: Aren't we going to the airport?

ABBY: No, they changed their plans. They're taking the train.

ME: (I pause for second to take in the change in plans) Let's get on the train everyone. Make sure you have your suitcases and any stuff you need for the ride.

(The families are now riding on the train. At this point, one of the babies comes up to the baby girl from my family and starts playing with her).

ABBY: Goo-goo. Gaga. Googoo.

ME: Gagagoogoo. Gagagoogoo.

ABBY: Hahahaha. Gaga. Gaga.

ME: Gaga. Gaga. Gaga. Hahahahaha!

ABBY: Hahahaha! Gaga. (Now Abby takes on the voice of the mother) come on now dear. Come over here, it's time for you to take a nap.

ME: (I take on the voice of the mother of my family) You too dear. Let's go, you can play with your friend a little later.

(The mothers put their respective babies down for a nap in the sleeper car.)

ABBY: Oh, I hear them. They're waking up now.

ME: Didn't they just fall asleep?

ABBY: No. It's been a few hours. They were very tired.

ME: Ok. I'm coming dear, I'm glad you had a chance to rest. (I go and retrieve my baby and return to the main car of the train.)

ABBY: That's not her you know (stated matter of factly).

ME: What?

ABBY: That's not her. That's not your baby. That's a different baby.

ME: (Here we go again, I think) A different baby.

ABBY: Yeah.

ME: What do you mean yeah! How can it be a different baby? I just got her from her crib (as I point to the pretend crib on the train).

ABBY: But she's different.

ME: She looks just like my baby. She's dressed like my baby. She sounds like my baby. She even smells like my baby!

ABBY: She's not your baby.

ME: You've got to be kidding.

ABBY: No. I already told you. I'm not. She was switched. That's a different baby. It may be her sister. Your baby is somewhere else now.

ME: But she doesn't have a sister.

ABBY: Yes she does. She was switched with her sister. They look alike. They're twins.

ME: But I need to find my baby (my voice is pressured, conveying my concern).

ABBY: You can't.

ME: (My voice rises plaintively) what do you mean, I can't! I have to! Conductor! Stop the train! Mr. Train guy! Can you help me? This isn't my baby! I don't know where my baby is! Please help!

ABBY: They won't be able to help you. They're too busy running the train and making sure everything is working. You'll have to find her yourself.

ME: But where can she be?

ABBY: Try looking around. Maybe you'll find her.

ME: (I search everywhere but come back with a defeated look on my face). I don't know where she is.

ABBY: Oh, that's her. She's back.

ME: But that's the same baby (as I enunciate every syllable for emphasis).

ABBY: No it isn't. She was switched back. That's your baby. The other baby is her twin sister and she's not here anymore.

ME: But how could she have a twin sister? Why didn't I know about it?

ABBY: It was a secret (Now Abby is over enunciating).

ME: (Sighs and turns to the baby in the crib). I'm just glad that you're back. I was looking all over for you. Are you ok? (I have the baby make some relieved baby noises).

ABBY: It's not her again.

ME: No.

ABBY: Sorry. That's the sister again.

ME: But I've been here the whole time.

ABBY: (In a bland almost bureaucratic voice) She was switched. She's disappeared again.

ME: Noooo!

I would love to say that it was clear to me how Abby was working out her own early experiences of loss and the confusion of having been adopted. I would also love to say how her play reflected how she both longed for and dreaded a chance to reconnect to her biological parents. I would also love to say I had a handle on the myriad sibling issues that were being played out in this little snippet, not to mention the questions of identity and self that Abby was trying to work out. But I didn't. All I knew was that I was playing multiple parts of a family that was constantly changing and being replaced while on an unpredictable train ride to some unknown part of the world. I was confused and getting increasingly frustrated. So, I tried to get some control back.

ME: (In an angry tone) She couldn't have been switched. It's impossible.

ABBY: But I told you she was (in the calmest of voices).

ME: Prove it. I was watching her the entire time and I know for a fact that she is the same baby who was in my arms. In fact, I don't think I even put her down since she woke up from her nap. She was not replaced.

ABBY: I'm sorry. That's not the same baby.

ME: I have with me a certificate of her birth that includes her eye color, hair color, and recognizable features to identify her. It says here there is a birthmark on her right forearm and you can see there is the same birthmark on this baby's arm. (I looked at Abby most triumphantly).

ABBY: (She looks right back at me with indifference) they look exactly the same. That's not her.

After failing to change the storyline, I took another approach to return the play to a more comfortable and straightforward place.

ME: (I adopt a voice of authority) I'm the conductor. I'm here to investigate the missing baby. We think we know where she is.

ABBY: What do you think you're doing?

ME: I'm the conductor.

ABBY: No you're not.

ME: I am. Here is my conductor's badge.

ABBY: Let me see. Boom! There was an accident. The conductor is dead.

ME: He can't be.

ABBY: Let me check his breathing. He's not breathing. He's dead. You'll have to find the baby yourself now.

ME: Wait, I'll call the assistant!

ABBY: Vroom! None of the phones work here.

ME: It can't be. There has to be a way to contact someone who can help!

ABBY: Sorry. There isn't.

After giving in to the fact that my baby had been switched, my next idea in our play was to have some outside people help me find her. There are times when adding a new character to a play can be very helpful, as it offers a new approach or persona that can broaden the play. To the extent that characters can represent different parts of oneself, adding a new one can help enrich the play by presenting a part of a child's self or representing a figure in a child's life who may otherwise remain underrepresented. That was my thinking at this part of the play but Abby would have none of it, her response incredulous as she swiftly disposed of my new characters.

So much of my work with Abby had been about letting go. I had accepted her need to tell me what to do and to remark on my incompetence. I had to let go of making too many comments or asking too many questions, thinking first about how Abby would respond. I had even let go of my name. In truth, these were all relatively easy, as they were all conscious and deliberate decisions that I had made about how to proceed. As Abby's stories developed though, the challenge grew, as I was now flying blind, not knowing the meaning of Abby's play or being able to anticipate what was going to happen next in our sessions. My power struggle with Abby over the baby switching, not to mention my use of terms such as *recognizable features* with a six-year-old, points to how hard a time I was having. Without question, one of the most challenging aspects of child therapy is tolerating moments of play or for that matter conversation that appear either irrelevant or that zigzag to the point of bewilderment. As adults, we tend to speak in a linear fashion and adults who don't comply are generally diagnosed as psychotic unless they are among the fortunate few to be deemed extremely creative. When working with children, who may experience the world in a more spontaneous and open fashion, there is a strong pull to make sure that stories and ideas make sense, in an adult-like fashion. To make the point stronger, I've spent the first part of this discussion talking about how happy I was to see Abby's play become more organized and linear. That said, there is a point where the play, or the conversation, can take a different turn and where the therapist, or for that matter any adult, needs to take a leap of faith to join the child in his or her world.

This leap is incredibly challenging. It can also be absolutely critical if one is going to enter into a child's world, where anything is possible. This leap allows for such fantastical adventures and figures. It allows for Snoopy, a beagle who thinks he's a heroic fighter pilot, and Winnie, a bear who for some reason goes by the name Pooh, and lives in a forest with a rabbit, a giraffe, and something called a Heffalump. It allows for a sea sponge and a starfish to become best friends while making up silly songs, consuming alarming amounts of junk food, and occasionally saving the deep from a demented piece of plankton. It allows for an orphan boy named Harry to realize he's a chosen wizard and a hero. In other words, this most difficult leap is also incredibly thrilling and magical.

I wished I had responded to Abby's play on the train differently. If I had just gone along with the plot, I could have learned and explored so much more about Abby's ideas and feelings regarding her own family switch. But, my desire for clarity got the best of me. Luckily, children can be quite forgiving and despite my missteps, I didn't have to wait long to resume the play. Abby walked back into my office the following week, told me what toys to get out of the closet, and we were right back on the train. I was traveling with my children, who were being switched on me yet again. This time I knew better than to fight the storyline. I allowed my character to desperately seek out her child and deal with the constant switching and craziness of the trip. For the next few weeks, we returned to this theme and continued to play out the story of the missing child. I had considered a variety of hypotheses concerning the play. Was Abby playing out the experience of displacement she sometimes felt as an adopted child? Was she identifying with her biological mother and trying to understand and justify how someone could give her up? Was this about her adopted mother who struggled to understand her and worried about Abby's ultimate interest in her biological or "real" parents?

Abby's tantrums and her ability to tolerate frustration at home had both improved, as had her relationships with other children. Some of that came from her mom's feeling better about ignoring Abby's outbursts while focusing on enjoyable experiences they could share to build their relationship, and some of it came from our work together. However unclear the precise meaning of the play, Abby was definitely expressing her feelings about her past and her very powerful need for control in the present. The more control I gave Abby in our sessions, the more control she displayed outside of them.

I still wanted to know what was going on in our sessions, though. Certainly, some of my annoyance came from my own desire to know and understand, but I started to look at my frustration as a clue. Maybe I needed to feel lost and estranged. Maybe that's how Abby felt at times, as she struggled to make sense of her own history and her own unrootedness. Perhaps the whole point of her young life had been learning to deal with the unexpected. Did it make sense that Abby had been born to a mother she did not know, in a country on the other side of the world? Did it make sense that somehow she went from a little village in Romania to New York City, where a new person adopted her and became her mother? Did it make sense that there was another girl, just a few years older, who had the same experience and was now Abby's sister? Maybe that's what I needed to get used to.

I realized that it was time to put my own lack of clarity in perspective. These rather wild stories, made up by Abby, were not meant primarily to confuse me. They were in fact reflections of Abby's own confusion. She was the one who had been switched and who had to get used to a different parent and a mysterious sibling. She was the one who had traveled great distances on her journey toward a new family. And she was the one who had to make sense of it all. And maybe, that's exactly what she was trying to do with me in our sessions.

I also thought about how much fun I was having with Abby. For a child who was so controlling, she was also very spontaneous and her play was full of energy. I felt almost like family or a friend on a play date in our sessions. Perhaps this feeling was telling me about a void that Abby was trying to fill, very effectively in our sessions. In the train scene, my family had two parents, but Abby's had no father, paralleling the rest of her play, which only included maternal figures. Perhaps I was filling this role for Abby in our sessions. Abby and I had clearly carved out a special place in our play, as we engaged each other with great ease. Of course we bickered and annoyed each other at times, but who doesn't?

Echoing the changes in our relationship, Abby and I left the train scenes, with their separate families, and embarked on our next adventure, as the prince and princess of a kingdom. Back on the carpet, we used the castle, action figures, puppets, and emptied colored storage bins to create an imaginary kingdom that was ruled by a largely absent king and queen, but dominated by the relationship between the prince and the princess. The princess was quite good at currying favor with the king and queen, while she ordered the prince to help prepare the royal throne, fix lunch and dinner, and clean the palace. The prince of course protested, but to little avail, as the princess always had her way and the prince always got reprimanded. From time to time the princess offered the prince a bit of hope, allowing him to order around some of the palace guards, and occasionally letting him sit on the royal throne, but, the princess inevitably took away her presents, and scoffed at the prince's predictable cycle of emerging hope and ultimate frustration.

One day, the prince and the princess stopped their arguing and became allies. The king and queen were out of town and enemy forces were preparing to march on the castle. The princess was concerned, and turned to the prince for help. It so happened that Abby had brought in a collection of gummy bears, gummy worms, and sour patch kids to our session. The prince suggested forming an army from the candies, and the princess was delighted with the suggestion. With our lead as generals, the gummy bear army, sour patch kids tank forces, and gummy worm air submarine commanders easily dispatched the invaders and the kingdom was safe. The princess, feeling kindhearted to the prince, complimented him on his plan and recorded the events in the royal diary. Finally, the prince felt appreciated and welcome in the royal palace.

The princess's goodwill was short-lived. As soon as the king and queen returned to the palace, she told them what had transpired and took full credit for the battle plan and resulting victory. When the prince asked to read the royal diary, he found the entry had been changed, and his frustration grew once more. Despite this betrayal, the relationship between the prince and princess was beginning to change, and the princess continued to intermittently compliment and befriend the prince. Meanwhile, in the real world outside of our sessions, Abby went on a vacation to England with her mother and sister. One of the highlights of her trip was eating and purchasing Smarties, England's version of M&M's. Abby came to session wearing an incredibly wide smile while holding aloft an immense plastic tube of the candy, which she proceeded to share with me. I cannot fully describe how happy I was, having been given a few candy coated English chocolates by Abby, who was now seven years old. Wow, I thought, maybe things were changing.

In the ensuing weeks, Abby continued to feed me, bringing two snacks, one for each of us, to every session. We would begin our session with play, and at some point, she would check with me to make sure we had enough time to eat. The girl who used to boss me around was now caring for me, offering me cookies, brownies, and gummy bears. We would sit down and enjoy the sweets, as we made light conversation. Abby would usually ask for an extra piece of my snack, which I happily shared back, completing our circle of nurturance and of sharing.

Meanwhile, in our play, the princess began to share pretend gifts and candy with the prince, who accepted them, albeit warily, as he questioned the princess's motives and trustworthiness.

PRINCESS: Oh Prince, come, let us go for a picnic. I have the most delicious lunch for us today. I just ordered it from the kitchen. (Abby takes out the pretend kitchen and food toys and gets them together as we take our customary places on the carpet).

PRINCE: (In a dutiful voice) Of course your highness, I'll be there right away.

PRINCESS: Isn't this lovely brother? (She says with great cheer).

PRINCE: (Blandly) No, actually it isn't.

PRINCESS: (Remaining cheerful) Oh, come on now, try to enjoy the picnic.

PRINCE: Of course, (the Prince said through clenched teeth) it's wonderful.

PRINCESS: Oh, dear (as she scrunches her face). Have some soup.

Tired of the prince's attitude, the Princess decided to take matters into her own hands and consulted with a magician, who provided her with a spell that would make the prince like her.

PRINCESS: (Cheerful and smiling broadly) Come brother, it's time for lunch.

PRINCE: (I respond in a grumpy voice) Yeah, yeah. I'm here.

PRINCESS: Here, have some chicken and some spaghetti.

PRINCE: Thanks.

PRINCESS: Hmmm. (The Princess casts the spell). Isn't this good? (She smiles at me expectedly).

PRINCE: (The Prince is a bit disoriented for a moment) Why, umm, umm, yes, it's delicious. This is a fantastic lunch sister. Did you make all this yourself? It's amazing!

PRINCESS: Why yes, I did.

PRINCE: You are so talented Princess. I am so honored and lucky to have such a wonderful and talented sister.

PRINCESS: Oh, it's nothing (as she shrugs her shoulders). You just enjoy. (Abby giggles).

PRINCE: I don't remember enjoying myself this much in such a long time. You really have made a fine lunch.

PRINCESS: And what do you think about the dishes? I picked them out myself.

PRINCE: Oh, they're splendid. Absolutely incredible. (The Prince looks perplexed)

PRINCESS: What's wrong Prince?

PRINCE: I don't know. I just don't totally feel myself. Something strange is going on but I don't know what it is. Maybe it was something I ate.

PRINCESS: Oh don't bother, just eat your lunch.

PRINCE: (The spell begins to wear off and I look at Abby suspiciously). What's going on?

PRINCESS: Nothing. We're having lunch. You were just telling me how wonderful everything is.

PRINCE: I was telling you what?! (As my eyes grow wide)

PRINCESS: How much you're enjoying my lunch. (Big broad smile).

PRINCE: What are you smiling about?

PRINCESS: Nothing.

PRINCE: All right, what scheme are you up to this time? I know you. Something's going on.

PRINCESS: (Abby tells me that she's recast the spell). How do you feel now?

PRINCE: Terrific. Never felt better. This is such a great day. It's so nice to spend time with you sister. We have to do this more often.

PRINCESS: Yes we do brother. Would you like some tea?

PRINCE: That sounds like a fantastic idea.

PRINCESS: Yes (she smiles again) Thank you. Here you go. Which cup would you like?

PRINCE: Oh, whichever one you think is best.

PRINCESS: I'll give you the blue one. Here.

PRINCE: Thanks. Ummh. It's delicious. The finest tea I have ever tasted.

This went on for the next few sessions, as the princess continued to fool the prince by casting spells to make him like her, and the confused prince told the princess how wonderful she was, before reverting to his crabbier ways. While Abby's play continued her typical manner of tricking me, the relationship between the prince and the princess continued to evolve. But, why the tricks? Why not just keep treating the prince nicely?

On the other hand, why was I, as the prince, being so ornery? The princess was trying out a kinder and gentler way of dealing with the prince, who was rejecting her attempts to change. To make matters more confusing, outside of the play, I was completely accepting of Abby's desire to share and spend time with me. I didn't reject her snacks or her conversation. I welcomed them.

In the next phase of play, Abby and I alternated between being prince and princess or brother and sister. We were typical siblings, who at this point generally got along but occasionally clashed. Joining in our play, for the first time, was a decidedly present and engaged mother, who organized picnics, held court in the royal palace, and helped defuse any problems brewing between her children. Both brother and sister deferred to her and worked hard to stay in mom's good graces. For the first time, the siblings were now part of a family unit, guided by a mother who was clearly in charge, helpful, and fair in taking care of her two children. This theme paralleled Abby's mother's report of life at home, as Abby continued to improve with respect to her behavior, was easier to talk to, and most of all, was far more affectionate.

Proactively, Abby's mother decided, with my support, to move Abby to a more nurturing school environment that offered less pressure and more room for Abby to develop both emotionally and academically. Abby welcomed the move, ostensibly as she had a very favorable impression of her new school uniform, but on another level, as she was comforted by her mother's clear and strong efforts to offer her an appropriately nurturing environment in which to grow and learn. So all seemed quite lovely and peaceful in our little world of play. Mother and her children were happy; Abby was doing well at home and at school, while in our sessions we enjoyed the rhythm and richness of imaginative play. Things were moving along so well I started to wonder what else we needed to accomplish in our sessions. As usual, Abby would let me know that we still had work to do as we sat on the carpet to begin our latest meal as brother and sister.

ABBY: Come let's start eating. Do you want a sandwich or a piece of chicken? I'm going to have the chicken, and this yummy slice of cake.

ME: I'm not feeling that hungry. I think I'll go with the sandwich and maybe some fruit.

ABBY: (In an eager voice) you know who's back?

ME: Who?

ABBY: Why don't you try to guess?

ME: Oh come on. I'll never guess it. Just tell me.

ABBY: Ok. I'll give you a hint. Someone we haven't seen in a long time.

ME: I don't know.

ABBY: A really long time.

ME: I still don't know.

ABBY: He hasn't been back home in 12 years (Now she's smiling).

ME: (I look at her perplexed) 12 years? 12 years? (Now I look in disbelief, my mouth wide open) No! It can't be.

ABBY: Dad's back!

ME: When did he get here? And where has he been anyway?

ABBY: He said he would tell me later. He said he would explain everything to me.

ME: He hasn't said anything to me. I didn't even know he was back.

ABBY: (Abby looks at me with an understanding gaze) aw, don't be upset about that. Just be happy that he's home. It's been 12 months since we saw him the last time.

ME: You mean years. 12 years (I say this intently).

ABBY: Yeah, and I was one when he left. Now I'm 13. I was just a baby (she says this dreamily).

ME: Where is he anyway?

ABBY: He's getting ready to go. We're going to Disney for a year by the way. Sorry, you can't come.

ME: Why not? I'm part of the family!

ABBY: Yeah. I know. Sorry, we'll be back in a year.

ME: How can you stay there for a year. You have to go to school.

ABBY: I am. I'm going to Disney school. Ha ha ha!

ME: To do what, learn to act like Mickey Mouse?

ABBY: (She chuckles) It's school. Just like regular school, except Mickey's your teacher.

ME: What does Mickey teach?

ABBY: Math.

ME: How about Donald Duck, what does he teach?

ABBY: Reading.

ME: (Sarcastically) He can barely talk, how can he teach reading?

ABBY: He teaches reading. Come on everybody, we've got to go. Make way!

So, a father figure was finally introduced. I remembered our early sessions about the trains and how my family had a father but Abby's never did. Not anymore. The sister, having been so young when he left, felt closer to her father, while the brother, my character, had grown distant, having been old enough to experience the pain of 12 missing years. There are so many ways to look at this vignette. I prefer to focus on how beneath all the confusion and trickery, Abby managed to weave in a completely new storyline involving the father, and his long and mysterious absence. In spite of the themes of abandonment and rejection, the sister is open for a rapprochement, echoing Abby's burgeoning capacity to deal with her own history.

Abby stayed on this theme for a few sessions, as I struggled to find the rest of my family, with intermittent moments of success, such as when I managed to get on a flight to Disney and found them, and of course, ultimate failure, such as when I was subsequently expelled from Disney for not having the proper paperwork.

These sessions offered Abby room to explore, with me, the different feelings and wishes that emerged as she pondered her history and her place in her old and her new families. Her bossiness had by now almost completely disappeared from our sessions. I felt very connected to Abby, as we explored her roots, her feelings of displacement and belonging, and her wishes to both connect with her history and stay focused on her present family. Abby's mother and I met and we again discussed the need for continued therapy. We decided that as Abby was exploring some heady themes, we would continue as she seemed to benefit and while her themes were at this point internal, those psychological dimensions were quite important to her development. At the same time, we also spoke about the possibility that Abby, who was reaching the age when many children begin to realize that they're actually going to see a therapist, would at some point begin to balk at coming to her sessions. The last time I had thought about ending, Abby introduced a father character. Now I wasn't sure if we were going to wind down or if Abby would bring up something entirely new.

She did both.

For the first time in two years, Abby used our sessions to play out rather typical everyday situations that she encountered at school, fantasy and metaphors not included. Our setting switched to an imagined school, and the main characters included a very bossy group of popular girls, a mean gym teacher, and a moody principal. These sessions were probably most interesting in that they were so reality-based and so easy to understand, likely reflecting a developmental shift that Abby was going through, as she began to move away from the world of fantasy and make-believe toward a world that maintained a sense of imagination, but was anchored in a more linear reality. Or, to be less arcane, Abby was saying goodbye to a land of fairy princesses and princes, and hello to the everyday world of school and its various pressures. We were able to deal directly with fitting in, popularity, and some burgeoning issues of cliques and meanness among classmates. There were the usual semi-comic moments when one of my characters would typically have the rug pulled out from under her, but otherwise, the play was oddly clear. I certainly felt more grounded than usual, but there was something missing from our play. It didn't have the same creative energy or magical quality that characterized our previous sessions. After all this time, I now missed being confused. In any event, summer was approaching, Abby was off to sleep-away camp, and her mother and I had planned a break for the summer and a resumption of sessions upon Abby's return in the fall.

But Abby had a different plan.

When I had said a few weeks earlier that Abby would one day let us know when she'd had enough therapy, I was thinking a few months. Instead, I got a call from Abby's mother that we had indeed gotten to that point sooner rather than later. She hadn't given any particular reason to leave; she just said she didn't want to come anymore. In my head, I went over our last session but came up with nothing, other than some annoyance by Abby that she had wanted a play date with a friend. That sort of thing happens all the time and certainly had never before been the precipitant for ending therapy. Abby's mother and I agreed that Abby would see me a few times, we'd see how Abby was feeling, and subsequently make a decision about therapy. If there was something I should have learned by then about Abby though, it was that my plans, however well intentioned and reasoned, had their limitations.

Abby came to the next session but we barely played. She drew a few pictures but that was it. There was no more play, or fantasy. I was no longer a prince, a sibling, a child, or a principal.

After this session, Abby complained bitterly about coming to her next session and her mother called me, asking for advice about how to proceed. I suggested that we continue our plan to meet for a couple more sessions, though I also felt strongly that Abby shouldn't end the therapy with a bad feeling of her therapy experience that may carry forward. I knew that whatever the decision, there could come a time in Abby's life when she might want to resume therapy, a choice that could be jeopardized were she to end our work negatively. On the other hand, I felt that Abby's history predisposed her to carrying a sense of loss as she grew older and I was concerned of her ending therapy in the midst of a drama centering on rejection and abandonment. I worried that in fact, Abby was trying to turn around something she had perhaps felt regarding her own separation from her parents. Most of all, I wondered, what had happened to our relationship, and how did it come crashing down so quickly?

Abby would return for another session, but with great difficulty, and she barely spoke to me. It was at our last scheduled appointment before the summer break and Abby was planning, with great enthusiasm, to attend overnight camp. I told her I realized her feelings about seeing me and coming to our appointments had changed, and that I hoped we could talk about that when she got back after the summer. I wished her a wonderful summer and hoped she'd have a great time riding horses and performing in the camp theatre. Two months earlier, Abby had talked to me excitedly about her camp plans and the activities she wanted to try. Now, she didn't say a word.

After the summer, I checked in with Abby's mother and heard that Abby had a wonderful summer, made lots of friends, and was very excited to begin school. I also heard that she had no plans of coming back to see me. So what was the right thing to do? Should I push for Abby to continue therapy and work through the resistance? Was her desire to leave a reflection of a critical aspect of loss that I needed to help Abby resolve so that she could engage in healthier relationships as she grew older? Could I possibly allow a child to make a decision about her own therapy? Wouldn't that be precisely the wrong thing to communicate to Abby, who to put it nicely, had control issues?

Resistance comes up in every therapy and often the best approach is to ride it out, and hope you come out on the other side with a relationship that has only been strengthened through adversity. If I stopped therapy every time a child protested, then the majority of the children I've worked with would have ended our work most prematurely. But sometimes, not listening to a child's voice can be a mistake, and in the process destructive. My decision would have been much easier if Abby had been struggling in school or had a disastrous summer camp experience. But she hadn't. She was thriving across the board. Perhaps, the best thing I could do was to allow her to end, with a proper goodbye, in a way that allowed Abby to save face and come back in the future if she so desired. I had ceded control to Abby so many times in the therapy. She had needed to control the beginning, middle, and now end of therapy. And I had learned that giving her that control had always been for the best. Abby, the child who had such little say over her own separation and loss, needed to have it at this important ending, and I needed to respect that. Maybe instead of engaging her in a battle of control, I needed to step back and respect her voice. Maybe that was precisely the resolution she had been working toward in the last few months of therapy.

My final session with Abby was difficult. Her mother and I agreed we would have a goodbye session after camp was over, which I felt was important despite the inevitable discomfort. I knew that it was hard for Abby to say goodbye and that she simply wished to not see me again. I also knew that under all this was a now eight-year-old girl who was feeling extremely vulnerable ending her therapy after working with me for two years. But a goodbye, however incomplete, was in order, as I wanted Abby to know that though I wished we could continue, I would not disappear or crumble as a result of her leaving. I would continue to be here in my office, wishing her well, and welcoming her back if she needed my support in the future. I would also stay with her in the confines of her own internal world, where we had spent so much of our time the past two years.

After buzzing Abby and her babysitter in for the last time, I came to get her from the waiting area. She was hiding behind her babysitter and didn't want to come in to my office. I told her that I understood, that I'd like her to come in, but that I would wait until she was ready. She wouldn't speak to me, so I decided to give Abby a little space and come back in a few minutes. About five minutes later, with the help of some coaxing from her babysitter, Abby came into my office. She sat down, but turned her head to the side. I spoke to her. I told her about the time we had spent together. How I remembered all the games we had played and the characters we had created. All the snacks we had shared, the Smarties, the cookies, and little tastycakes she used to bring for me. I remembered our time together as having been so enjoyable and meaningful. I told her I would always remember our sessions as special and would miss her as she went on to do other things, which I knew she wanted to do. I understood that the time had come for her to say goodbye and that saying goodbye was very hard to do.

Abby looked away, so I decided to be quiet and just sit with her a few minutes. She just stood there, her face down now instead of turned away. So I thought, there has to be something I could say or do to turn this thing around. I couldn't possibly let therapy just end like this. After a few minutes of flailing and failing, I thought back about our first sessions and how little I had to say, and how I had tried so hard to figure out what was going on in the therapy. I thought about the lessons I had learned working with Abby. How important it had been for me to give her space and ultimately, to become comfortable just not knowing. It was time for me to accept that therapy would in fact end this way, on Abby's terms, and I had to trust, perhaps foolishly, that there was a reason why it had to be this way. So a few minutes later I looked at my watch and I told Abby that our session was over and it was time to say our goodbye. With more than a little prodding from her babysitter, Abby handed me over a package. It contained a box and a decorative bushel of oversized lollipops. I thanked her. She looked to the floor. She was about to go, when I motioned to her with the lollipops. I asked her if she'd take one as I really had quite a few. She looked up a second, then back to the floor. She did this twice more before she tentatively walked over and looked over the pops as I held them for her. After deciding between different colors, she chose one and started to walk out. I said goodbye again and she turned back, lollipop in hand, and gave me a wave.

It wasn't the heartiest wave. In fact, it was rather weak. But, it was a wave and given how things had been progressing, I took that as little bit of light in the darker space of our ending. At least Abby had been able to look at me in the end, and say goodbye.

I sat down with my box and unwrapped it. It was a very lovely pen from Abby's mom. I thought for a few moments about the final session, about the past two months, and about the last two years of therapy. Abby and I had been on quite a journey. We had taken baffling train rides, played out a doomed fairy-tale romance between bears, and established a kingdom guarded by a sugarcoated army. And ultimately, we encountered parents, who had been so absent from the early sessions. In that time, Abby had gone from bossing me around, to tolerating me, to enjoying our time together, until she decided to leave. As for me, I had fully learned the importance and the power of joining Abby as her fellow traveler, wherever that meant winding up, instead of needing to know our destination. I had enjoyed the pleasure and the magic of our relationship and the creativity of our play, as we lost ourselves in imagination. As I sat there at the end of our final session, I figured one day I'd know what it all meant. Or, just as importantly, maybe I wouldn't. In the meanwhile, I did what felt most natural. I started to unwrap a large bright orange lollipop.

3 The Adventures of Captain Pineapple

"Psychotherapy takes place in the overlap of two areas of playing, that of the patient and that of the therapist. Psychotherapy has to do with two people playing together."

(Winnicott, 1971)

"The therapist does not attempt to direct the child's actions or conversation in any manner. The child leads the way; the therapist follows."

(Axline, 1947)

Winnicott's oft-quoted statement embraces the beauty of a therapeutic relationship, with therapist and child partnering to understand a child's world and tell a child's story. But, how does the therapist play? To what extent are a therapist's playful tendencies beneficial in therapy? Axline's well-known prescription offers the child a fundamental respect that is the basis for seeing therapy as a safe space in which a child explores his or her feelings, and with the therapist's help, tells his or her story. The child leads and the therapist follows. But, how does the therapist follow? Can the therapist still be quite engaged and even active while still following the child's lead? What if the therapist feels that therapy has hit a dead-end? What if a child can't play?

The quotes from Winnicott and Axline reflect a tension as to the place of a therapist's personality and therapeutic agenda in working with children. Beautiful examples abound across psychoanalytic, non-directive, and gestalt approaches that point to child therapy as a space where children are able to express themselves through play and/or words, and in the process work through unresolved conflicts, integrate different parts of themselves, and express feelings that have remained dormant. The therapist takes on characters at the child's request and sometimes even asks the child what his or her character should say or do before responding (Chethik, 2003). At times, the therapist may interpret or reflect on the child's thoughts or feelings, and while these comments are certainly active interventions, the therapist is expected to otherwise follow the child's lead. Some therapists go a step further and place themselves more squarely in the center of therapeutic work. For example, while emphasizing a child's telling of his or her story, clinicians such as Crenshaw (2006), Oaklander (1988), and Cattanach (1997) introduce activities or offer evocative stories designed to elicit specific emotional themes or experiences that resonate with a child. According to Crenshaw there may be times when a child's play may lose energy or veer off course, and a therapist's evocative play or storytelling enlivens the work. Van Fleet (2010) explains that following a child's lead refers not to passively following everything a child does but to following the child's intention and emotional expression. In that spirit, she encourages the therapist to be both playful and evocative in order to develop a therapeutic space that resonates with a child's emotional experience.

From a psychoanalytic perspective, aside from the clear agenda-setting of any interpretation, there has been interest in the spontaneous moments when a therapist "*breaches technique,*" by bringing more of him or herself into the room (Carlberg, 1997; Lanyado, 2004; Blake, 2011). Not surprisingly, interest in the therapist's use of play has been put forth by clinicians with a relational bent who highlight the role of unconscious communication in treatment. Emphasizing the importance of the therapeutic relationship, and echoing a particular interpretation of Winnicott's idea of two people playing together, Frankel (1998) and Blake (2011) speak about the importance of the therapist actively joining the child in play, as they highlight the role of the therapist's own personality and playfulness in engaging a child. Frankel talks of the importance of the therapist's personality as it shapes the nature of a given treatment, contrasting his own physically-active play with that of a colleague who may tend toward quieter dialogue-filled play with dolls or playhouses. Ferro (1999), focusing on the unique therapeutic space, or field, that develops between therapist and child, deepens emotional themes in a child's play by adopting various characters in response to a child's play or drawings, as he jumps into play as an actor and co-author of a child's story. While these approaches encourage the therapist's improvisation, a reticence to the use of the therapist's own creative play remains. Such hesitation is certainly understandable, as we seek to listen to each child so that we can help develop and raise his or her voice in our work. It is often by letting go and following a child that we are most able to help him or her (Kronengold, 2010).

But, what happens when a therapist decides to follow an instinct and initiates play with characters who may resonate with a child, either by representing important themes, people, or aspects of the child's own personality? What if the therapist decides to become a purposeful actor, maybe even director, of a child's story? What is the place for such an active stance in child therapy? Can the therapist's own creative play help a child by actively building a therapeutic space in which a therapist and child can work together? Or, perhaps the therapist's creativity is best kept in check, so as to avoid getting in the way of the natural unfolding of a child's emotional world.

Ethan, ten years old, sauntered into my office, pointing at books, toys, and a clock, not so much exploring as marking territory, his husky physique and booming voice matching the physicality of his entrance. His family lived in the suburbs of New York, about an hour from my office, and during Ethan's three-month summer break, contacted me for short-term work. The expectation was that I would work with Ethan briefly, help the family with ideas they could use at home, and offer suggestions that could be integrated into the therapeutic services he was receiving at school. Perhaps the consultative nature of this therapy influenced my decision to take more chances, but though our time together was brief, Ethan's influence on my thoughts has loomed large.

At the start of our work, Ethan's parents sent me a three-inch high stack of papers filled with previous evaluations, report cards, and school assessments. Ethan had come into this world with developmental challenges. He had struggled with speech, often misunderstanding the nuances of language used in everyday conversation, though he was quite adept at recounting large amounts of factual information. Ethan presented with sensory difficulties, as he became easily overwhelmed when a space was too loud, too crowded, or visually stimulating. Relationships were similarly challenging as Ethan struggled with compromise and tended to get focused on a particular area of interest not often shared by his peers. Ethan was also prone to upset at the slightest provocation, perceived insult, or change in routine – yelling, cursing, and hitting when upset. At his suburban school setting, Ethan's language and academic needs were supported by specialists, and he joined an after school group to work on developing his social skills. To help with the behavioral difficulties, Ethan also saw a psychopharmacologist for medication treatment. His parents hoped that I could work with Ethan and offer parenting help to better manage his behavior. From meeting and reading about Ethan, I came to see that the immensity of his reactions spoke to an internal experience that was too much for him to manage. For Ethan, sadness, frustration, and excitement, all feelings really, registered in big bright neon letters. There wasn't much of a middle ground, as Ethan often felt overwhelmed, much as he overwhelmed his parents and teachers. Looking down at the huge stack of papers before me, I understood the feeling.

Typically, my first meeting is with a child's parents, where I can get some history, and parents and I can decide whether to move forward. In Ethan's case I had plenty of history, and as part of the work included supporting the family, I wanted to see how he and his parents interacted. So, I decided to meet with them as a family, giving me a chance to talk with them about Ethan's behavior while also giving them room to play and interact. I realize that spending a session with me observing can be daunting for a family, as parents can feel as if they are being scrutinized for mistakes and flaws. With that in mind, Ethan's parents were open and brave to comfortably settle into my office. Ethan eyed me carefully. I encouraged them to start playing and they began to literally horse around; Ethan lay down on his father's back, while his father, who had gone on all fours, gave Ethan a pony ride through the office. What a sight it was, evoking both a sense of exhilaration at Ethan's joy as he laughed and shouted, "*Good horsie! Good horsie!*" and exhaustion, as his father ultimately tired and bent forward, while Ethan kept yelling for his "*horsie*" to keep going. Likewise, Ethan was all over his mother, as play with puppets quickly shifted to Ethan hugging and glee-fully jumping on his mother. From watching Ethan and his parents, it was clear that there was great love in this family. The challenge was going to be to help channel this love so that Ethan could begin to learn some of the boundaries and limits of expressing himself, and so his parents could love him while also letting him know when they had enough.

While Ethan looked impulsive from afar, his behavior took on more nuance once I engaged with him in play. In our first two sessions, I began to see that the slightest upset, a missing toy or schedule change, led Ethan to frustration, as he directed his anger at either his parents or me. He became upset when he couldn't find a piece from a toy or struggled to catch a ball. At the same time, Ethan was also very friendly, greeting me with a big smile and an enthusiastic hello. Even when he was furious, Ethan never sounded tough or threatening, a quality that helped make him approachable. It seemed so clear from his voice that he was extremely angry, but more than anything else, frustratingly disappointed and overwhelmed. I started to con-nect Ethan's upset with the occurrence of anything that was unexpected – his frustration tied to his need for order and predictability.

We all have to shift gears in dealing with the world. If I go to my closet to pick out a shirt and it's in the laundry, then I have to find something else to wear. If I head to the subway, and there's a delay, I need to decide whether to walk, take a bus, or jump in a taxi. We all face these sorts of decisions, predicated on the disruption of our plans, many times a day. For some chil-dren, including Ethan, these situations are intensely difficult, as changes in plan are as fingernails on a chalkboard.

Some ten-year-olds express themselves verbally, some through play, while many shift between the two. In our first meetings it was clear to me that Ethan was definitely in the playing category, so I decided to start with building, an activity Ethan loved. We began with *Widgets*, geometric blocks that Ethan's mother had told me were a favorite and which Ethan brought in to show me. The blocks come with pattern cards that give the child a model of what to build. Ethan made quick work of these, assembling the different patterns in record time. His work was certainly impressive, but I was interested to see how he could respond to a new challenge, as *Widgets*, though a wonderful toy, is nothing if not predictable, and I wanted, through our play, to help expand Ethan's flexibility. At the same time that I wanted to challenge Ethan, I also wanted to stay in an area of comfort, so as not to overwhelm him. I shifted to blocks and Lego for more free-form building, allowing Ethan to stay within his strong set of building skills while at the same time introducing the challenge of building without a template. I had expected Ethan to resist the change, but he took this challenge well. When building with blocks or Lego, Ethan worked quietly and skillfully, using an architect's eye to erect stunningly exact and symmetrical buildings. There was beauty in his work.

There was also so much vulnerability. What would happen if one piece went askew? What if the sides didn't match? Would the loss of order and structure lead to disaster? I also noticed that Ethan's buildings were perfectly still – no people, family life, or bustle – and as he built, his focus was so intense that I felt I didn't much exist in the room.

In fairness, I had also asked Ethan to manage a task without a template, and in response he had managed to tolerate the ambiguity and constructed some beautiful pieces. As for Ethan shutting me out of this part of the building, well, to be perfectly fair, I knew Ethan struggled with his relationships, and the two of us were just getting acquainted. Rather than judging Ethan, I preferred to use my feeling of being left alone as an impetus to join him in the play rather than staying in my safe role on the periphery. I admit to my own anxiety, as I expected to draw the ire of this child who relied so heavily on familiarity and control. I didn't want Ethan to scream at me. I also didn't want to sit in my office feeling disconnected while I watched him build each session. I wondered about my desire to more actively connect with him. With another child, I might have been more patient but not with Ethan. Why? Perhaps I was being too hasty. Maybe if I followed his building, perhaps playing parallel to Ethan or commenting on his work, he would gradually allow me entrance into his world. But, while other children had orchestrated play and kept me at a distance, I typically felt a certain emotional resonance to the play and to my frustration. With Ethan, the feeling was different – I felt cut off. I was very much an audience and I expected that without intervention on my part, I would likely watch him build the same structure for the next three months. So, as I sat next to him on the carpet, and watched Ethan survey the room, I suggested we build together. Ethan ignored me twice. I moved a touch closer, tapped Ethan on the shoulder, cleared my throat, and repeated myself. Ethan gave me an annoyed look before finally responding.

ETHAN: Where are the Legos?

ME: They're in the closet.

ETHAN: I want them! (His shoulders stiffen, as his voice gets higher)

ME: (I think for a moment whether to follow Ethan or challenge him. I choose a compromise) Ok. They're right over that way (I said cheerfully, as I point to the closet while wondering how this will turn out).

ETHAN: I want them now! Get them!

ME: Great, they're right over there (I motion to the closet). Just walk right over and we can start playing with them (which I say a bit too breezily at this point).

ETHAN: Get them for me!!!

ME: Uh-uh (I shrug, working to stay relaxed).

ETHAN: (Sounding very frustrated and struggling to hold it together) But I want them and I want you to get them!

ME: (I wait for a moment before I'm ready to speak in a voice that is clear but engaging. I had been feeling tense and realize I need to relax, otherwise Ethan would pick up on my discomfort and probably become overwhelmed). I know you're annoyed and I realize that I'm upsetting you right now. Here's the thing (my voice lowers slightly, as I lean in slightly and use my hands to gesture). I think you can get the Lego without me. I'm pretty sure, actually. But, I don't want to fight, so I have an idea. Why don't we walk over there together (I gesture to the closet) and we'll get the Lego?

ETHAN: But I'm tired!

ME: It's not really that far you know.

ETHAN: Yes it is, don't tell me that!!!

ME: (I look at Ethan for a moment, his face now red with frustration. I think about what to do. Not thinking of anything particularly helpful to say, I look straight at Ethan and put my hand on his shoulder, which responds to my touch and starts to soften). Come, let's go to the closet and get some blocks. We really don't need to fight.

ETHAN: (His voice calmer and more vulnerable) I think we do.

ME: Of course we don't (I say calmly again as I see Ethan settle down. Then I decide to add a little humor to our exchange and begin to speak in an exaggerated tone). Yelling at me about Lego! C'mon! (I start to walk with Ethan to the closet) I mean, I like Lego, you like Lego. They're interconnecting blocks – what's not to like, right?

ETHAN: (Walks with me but lets out a harrumph). Oh, man.

Children and adults either became afraid of Ethan or tried to put him in his place, just fueling his anxiety and explosiveness. Of course, most of the people in Ethan's life did not appreciate this anxiety, mistaking him as simply impulsive and combustible, when much more was going on underneath the surface. Ethan had gotten angry and was starting to boil as I refused to get him the toys. I could have acquiesced, doing his bidding and perhaps reflecting on his wishes, or I could have tried to set a clear limit, telling Ethan what I would and would not do, while challenging him to cope. I might have chosen either of these approaches at another time in our work, but at that moment I wanted most of all to join Ethan. I chose a different route, trying to meet Ethan halfway, as I worked to modulate my voice, at times going higher to match Ethan and at times lower to calm him, and body language, a hand on his shoulder, to engage Ethan. With another child, such a move could be highly intrusive, but I already knew from my first session with Ethan and his family that he found comfort and a language in physical closeness. A hand on the shoulder meant I was letting Ethan know that I wasn't scared of him but was comfortable and ready for a journey. In the process, Ethan relaxed, and as we walked to the closet, he emerged as a rather large and sensitive bear of a boy, rather than an out-of-control whirlwind. We took out the Lego, did some building, and Ethan started telling me about the universe. He talked to me and shared his great knowledge about space, teaching me about various moons and stars with an emphasis on Triton and Charon, his favorites. I was grateful to learn about Ethan's world.

In our next session, we again took out the blocks and started building. Ethan resumed building the same structure from the previous session. It can be tricky to decide when to follow such play. Sometimes, a child will repeat play to gain mastery or work through feelings or concerns, and sometimes repetition is a defense where a child may continue the same play to avoid certain feelings. For other children, the repetition is part of their developmental challenge. I have no doubt that building spoke to Ethan on an emotional level. He was at peace when working with Lego or blocks. But, his play wasn't yet symbolic. There were no themes or characters in his play. Ethan also didn't use play to enjoy another person's company. Rather, building brought Ethan a self-focused and repetitive calm. Instead of focusing on the symbolism of the buildings, I turned to a different set of questions – How could Ethan manage change in his routine? Could he integrate new characters and challenges in the play? Could he begin to tell stories? Most importantly, could he integrate me into his play to allow the work to become truly interactive? Only in that way could Ethan begin to make strides in dealing with other children and adults in his life.

In thinking about helping Ethan, the continuation of Winnicott's quote about two people playing together comes to mind – "The corollary of this is that where playing is not possible the work done by the therapist is directed towards bringing the patient from a state of not being able to play into a state of being able to play." Of course, how a therapist helps a child become able to play is open to interpretation. I was trying to use an active approach to help expand Ethan's ability to tell stories, understand feelings, and allow me into his world – to help Ethan develop an internal space in which he could begin to deal with both feelings and other people. As we sat down with Lego, I made building suggestions, helped out as an assistant, and when nothing else succeeded, made comments or asked Ethan questions about his creations. My comments were by turn complimentary, noticing the impressiveness of Ethan's work, inquisitive, wondering about his pattern and building choices, and a bit impish, as when I suggested the use of a particularly impressive Palladian-like structure as a bowling alley. I noticed that compliments and questions didn't elicit much from Ethan other than a shrug or a monosyllabic response. My humorous comments on the other hand elicited a reaction, as we started to talk about and debate his building designs. Choosing to introduce a human element into his play, I went to my toy closet and brought out my puppets along with assorted little Lego guys, led by a dreadlocked, Jamaican-accented bird puppet, known as Pookie.

POOKIE: This place is amazing! Hey, Hello there, what a great place to live (I turn to the Lego people and wave them over). This is going to be fantastic guys! Everyone, come on! (I have the Lego guys follow Pookie as they murmur excitedly).

ETHAN: (Ethan looks aghast) These are my buildings!

POOKIE: And you've done a great job! These are really beautiful! What's your name, man?

ETHAN: Ethan.

POOKIE: Very pleased to meet you. My name is Pookie. You have heard of me, perhaps?

ETHAN: No, never have.

POOKIE: (Sighs) Oh well. Anyway, great job building. Excuse me. (Yells out to the rest of the gang) Come on everybody, we're going to live in Ethan's apartment buildings!

ETHAN: No way! You are not living here!

POOKIE: Don't worry. It will be a blast. You know, we will always honor you – Our builder!

ETHAN: Hold it. You can't live here. I built these buildings! They're just for me! Not you!

POOKIE: You don't want us here?

ETHAN: No, I don't!

POOKIE: Really?

ETHAN: Yes!

POOKIE: It's because I'm a puppet isn't it?

ETHAN: No, it's not because you're a puppet.

POOKIE: Because if it is, I don't think you're being fair.

ETHAN: It's not because you're a puppet!

POOKIE: You're angry now. I can sense that.

ETHAN: No, I'm not angry. You're not supposed to live here! This is my building. I built it!

POOKIE: You're shouting at me.

ETHAN: Yes, you're annoying me!

POOKIE: Me annoying? (Pookie's mouth is open as he expresses his amazement and is speechless for a moment). Come my friend. (Pookie puts what he has of a wing around Ethan's shoulder). I think we should discuss an arrangement man.

ETHAN: What kind of arrangement?

POOKIE: You and me man! We shall live in this building, together! (Pookie says the last word with emphasis, his wing on Ethan's shoulder, his eyes peering up at the sky).

ETHAN: (Sighs) Oh boy.

Humor softened our exchanges, providing a safety that helped temper Ethan's sensitivity. The turning point in this sequence came when Pookie put his wing around Ethan's shoulder, as Ethan relaxed, echoing our earlier Lego interaction. My message through Pookie was that I saw Ethan as approachable, and yes, even lovable. After all, Pookie and his friends didn't just want to live in Ethan's buildings, but they wanted to honor, celebrate, and even hang out with Ethan, their master builder and hoped-for friend.

I wanted to play with Ethan and get to know him and I wondered how often Ethan got that message from people in his life.

As the play moved forward, Pookie continued to make appearances. Although Ethan found him a bit annoying, he also learned to manage and enjoy his puppet companion. In the meanwhile, Ethan's parents reported that he was more engaging and less explosive at home. I wondered why. Was my active play stance working, helping develop a space where Ethan could engage the world with a measure of greater openness and flexibility? Was it my stance toward him, my belief that Ethan could be a good friend that was helping? Or, as happens sometimes, was I just fortunate to have started work as he entered into a relatively calm place? One can never be sure, but I felt the play was beneficial as Ethan had become more open to my joining him. We had a rhythm going. As Ethan and I would build, Pookie would say something funny, and we'd enjoy ourselves. I wondered whether this was precisely what Ethan needed for the time being – to engage with me and learn to share his world with another person. He had been doing well. On the other hand, I was concerned that our play was going to lose its energy and freshness, as Ethan's play could easily become repetitive. So I decided to keep the play moving.

Ethan and I were playing with Lego and discussing space. I started building a spaceship and Ethan followed my lead, as we compared shipbuilding notes. As usual, Ethan built a beautifully detailed starship, while I mixed together a haphazard design that more closely resembled a rowboat with wings. I included a Lego man as ship commander and to make the character a bit more colorful plunked a Lego tree shrub on the ship commander's head as a helmet. Our play began.

ETHAN: My ship is protecting the Earth.

ME: (I think for a moment about whether to protect Earth at Ethan's side but decide this could be an opportunity to explore how Ethan deals with conflict. I choose to play a bad guy attacking Earth and adopt a standard evil villain voice.) Not for long my friend. I shall soon take over and rule the Earth.

ETHAN: No! No! No! You will not do any such thing. You will be destroyed!

ME: Guess again my friend. I shall rule Earth and the entire galaxy! Ha Ha Ha Ha Ha!!

ETHAN: No, I will destroy your ship!

ME: Destroy my ship? Destroy my ship! Do you have any idea who you're talking to here?

ETHAN: Do you have any idea who you're talking to?

ME: May I remind you that I asked you first, my soon to be conquered flying friend.

ETHAN: I'm not telling who I am. You tell me.

ME: Oh, but it won't matter my friend. You see, the Earth shall be mine! Ha Ha Ha Ha Ha!!!

ETHAN: No!!! No!!! You will be destroyed!!!

ME: Silly Earth people prepare to be conquered! Very well. Allow me to introduce myself. I am … I am … (Ethan looks at me expectedly. I'm trying to think of a good name. I quickly scan the room for inspiration, come up with nothing, but see my Lego figure's tree shrub hat and associate to an image from my childhood of Punchy, from the Hawaiian Punch commercials.) I am Captain Pineapple, your next ruler!!! Soon, the Earth shall be mine! Mine! All mine! (I break into a little song.) Who's going to take over the Earth? – Captain Pineapple! Who's going to take over the Earth? That's right! Uh-huh! Captain Pineapple!

ETHAN: You will not succeed Captain, ummm (Ethan looks at me for help).

ME: Pineapple.

ETHAN: Captain Pineapple. You will not take over the Earth! Never!!!

ME: Oh you silly earthling. You have no idea. Ha ha ha ha ha!

While the name and a few details may have been improvised in a moment of need, the idea of a Captain Pineapple-type of figure was in line with my thoughts about our play. I was looking to expand Ethan's flexibility by helping him deal with the unexpected. As a playfully kooky agent of chaos, Captain Pineapple wouldn't accept exactly what Ethan wanted but instead would challenge him. Ethan often struggled with others, becoming upset and confrontational. I decided to work from within this difficulty, thinking that dealing with Captain Pineapple might give us a chance to work on some of Ethan's everyday upset, as Ethan often encountered situations where he felt as if he was dealing with an awful villain. My hope was that Ethan would adapt, learn to understand, and negotiate with Captain Pineapple as a proxy for dealing with the rest of the world.

I also purposely chose a character whom I thought would resonate, and in the process help contain Ethan's impulsivity and upset. Captain Pineapple's over the top personality echoed aspects of Ethan's. In our work, we may comment about a child's aggression or other feelings to help make those feelings more manageable, as the therapist conveys an understanding that allows a child to better digest and understand his or her feelings. Sometimes just being with a child in a moment of upset can help make those feelings more manageable, as it is our very presence that helps a child contain difficult feelings. I had not had, nor did I anticipate having, success in talking with Ethan about his feelings at this time in our work. Our work was through action and play. I had been successfully conveying an understanding nonverbally – using my voice and body language to at times soothe and match Ethan's emotional state. Now, I wanted to use the play not just to understand, but also to give voice to the part of Ethan that became frustrated and aggressive. I wanted to use Captain Pineapple to venture into deeper places than Ethan could usually tolerate so that he could play with his feelings rather than just act upon them.

My intention was to introduce this character and then develop him, layering more complex emotions, motivations, and even a back-story that would help Ethan develop a map that he could use to understand his own emotional world. What drove Captain Pineapple? What did he feel when he concocted his outrageous plans? How did he deal with failure, particularly when the stakes were so high? Where did he come from anyway and why was he so fascinated with Earth? Were there any problems in his own galaxy? Did he have a family? What did his mother think about what he was doing?

I also wondered about introducing Captain Pineapple. The idea of the therapist helping a child hold onto and digest intolerable feelings has been highlighted across therapeutic schools of thought, with Winnicott's idea of holding and Bion's containment coming to mind. But how does one contain these feelings so that a child may play rather than act upon them? Barrows (2002), Kaduson (2006), and Gallo-Lopez (2005), all coming from different perspectives, encourage the therapist to become at times more clearly active and playful when the therapist feels closed out of the child's world. Barrows talked of the therapist's need to make contact with certain children using a more robust approach to play that includes introducing characters and themes into the work. In particular, he talks of taking on the role of a child's aggression and giving voice to it in a way that offers a child an opportunity to work on aggressive feelings that are otherwise intolerable. He describes a case where he took on the role of a shark and pretended to have the shark start biting the child. Similarly, Kaduson encourages the therapist to playfully create characters who may resonate with a child, particularly when the child is having difficulty playing or expressing certain feelings or experiences that may have proved especially painful. In one example, she acts out the role of a character who has witnessed a traumatic event in order to help a child begin to play with and ultimately talk about a similar experience that brought him into therapy. Gallo-Lopez's drama therapy fills the therapeutic space with a spirit of improvisation, as she offers the example of a therapist switching places with the child, who becomes the therapist while the therapist plays a sullen and angry teenager.

But, these examples notwithstanding, this sort of character play isn't typical in the literature. Perhaps I was overreaching? Why not make Captain Pineapple an ally rather than a foe? Pookie had been a bit annoying but in wanting to spend time with Ethan pulled for Ethan's desire for closeness and allowed Ethan to feel desirable. Captain Pineapple on the other hand, well, he was trying to defeat Ethan and conquer Earth. Would Pineapple actually help Ethan with his aggressive feelings, or would he instead set off Ethan's frustration and rigidity, leading Ethan to become aggressive and disorganized?

CAPTAIN PINEAPPLE: I'm back silly Earthling.
ETHAN: Don't call me silly. I'm going to get you Captain Pineapple!

CAPTAIN PINEAPPLE: I don't think so my friend. You see, you have no chance. I am Captain Pineapple, and I shall now begin my genius plan to take over the planet. Soon all shall bow to Pineapple. Ahh! It's going to be so cool!

ETHAN: No it won't Captain Pineapple. I'm going to stop you! You will not take over Earth! And it's not going to be cool!

CAPTAIN PINEAPPLE: Oh whatever, Earthling person. Now it's off to begin my plan (like all good villains I choose to then share far too much detail with Ethan about how I am going to conquer Earth. This both allows me to stay in character and to give Ethan a bit of exercise and success in fending off my plans). I'm off to Earth's largest marshmallow factory in Pittsburgh, Pennsylvania! That's where I will steal the Earth's supply of marshmallows and use them to power my super laser device. Once my super laser is operational, Earth will have no choice but to surrender to me, Captain Pineapple! (There is a long pause, as Ethan and I look at each other.) Hmmm. Maybe I didn't need to actually say all of that out loud.

ETHAN: (pauses for a moment to take in the information) Ha Captain Pineapple! You made a mistake! I know your plans, you fool! Now I'm definitely going to stop you!

CAPTAIN PINEAPPLE: Guess again silly Earthman! I cannot be stopped. And (I allow my voice to crack a tiny bit to convey vulnerability), don't call me a fool. That hurts my feelings. Your planet is mine! Off I go, shifting into hyper speed. Farewell Earth guy!

ETHAN: Not so fast Captain. Hyper speed now!

CAPTAIN PINEAPPLE: Hey, how did you do that? I'm the only one who has come up with hyper speed!

ETHAN: No you're not. I have it too.

CAPTAIN PINEAPPLE: Really, where did you get it?

ETHAN: From our space program. All of our ships have it.

CAPTAIN PINEAPPLE: Really, all of them?

ETHAN: Yes.

CAPTAIN PINEAPPLE: Wow. Impressive. Hmmm. What else do you have on your ship?

ETHAN: A super laser!

CAPTAIN PINEAPPLE: Super, but not super duper!

ETHAN: No, we have that too.

CAPTAIN PINEAPPLE: Ok. But do you have a deflector shield?

ETHAN: Yes, of course.

CAPTAIN PINEAPPLE: Tractor beam?

ETHAN: Yes.

CAPTAIN PINEAPPLE: Popcorn machine?

ETHAN: What?

CAPTAIN PINEAPPLE: Popcorn machine. Do you have a popcorn machine? I have just installed the new Super Popcorn Popper 18,000! Looks like you're outmatched Earthling guy!

ETHAN: I don't need a popcorn machine on a spaceship!

CAPTAIN PINEAPPLE: Sure you do.

ETHAN: What are you going to do with a popcorn machine?

CAPTAIN PINEAPPLE: Why, eat popcorn, foolish Earthling!

ETHAN: That's ridiculous! What's so great about your popcorn popper anyway?

CAPTAIN PINEAPPLE: It tastes better!

ETHAN: That's a ridiculous thing to have on a spaceship. That won't help you.

CAPTAIN PINEAPPLE: (over enunciating each word) so we shall see my old friend.

Sometimes you just play. It is that very fun, that meeting of a child and therapist in moments of great enjoyment, and indeed silliness, that can offer some of the most therapeutic of our experiences in working with children (Carlberg, 1997; Frankel, 1998; Blake, 2011). I realize these snippets may appear to be, well, honestly, nutty and perhaps self-indulgent. What was the point of these ridiculous ideas? Did I have to keep calling Ethan *Earthling guy*? I was going to take over a marshmallow factory? The Super Popcorn Popper 18,000?

Humor kept the play from overwhelming Ethan, who sometimes fought Captain Pineapple not so much as a play villain but a real one. It was at these times that our play ceased and Ethan may as well have been fighting an actual bad guy. I imagined that Ethan approached daily challenges in a similar manner – as each upset may have felt threatening, leading Ethan to defend himself. While I wanted Ethan to become emotionally engaged in our work, so that our play could capture his intense feelings, I did not want Ethan to become so frustrated that his anger made him unreachable. Captain Pineapple's comic book banter and kookiness, his remarkable popcorn machine, were important as they kept Ethan safely tethered to a sense of play. Remaining in a world of imagination allowed Ethan a therapeutic space to explore his feelings.

My goal with Captain Pineapple was to approximate yet contain Ethan's feelings. Ethan's explosiveness would appear with great intensity and seemingly little warning, But, I knew that a sequence of spiraling anger, sadness, and frustration was the recipe to his tantrums. In playing out Captain Pineapple's reactions, I made sure to slow the process down at moments, capturing the different steps along Pineapple's upset. The Captain made plenty of mistakes, impulsively blurting out his plans and getting angry with himself before turning his annoyance to Ethan. Captain Pineapple articulated his building frustration, and in doing so was working as an alter ego to help Ethan contain and understand his own reactions. Our containment of a child's aggressive feelings and our invitation to the child to play with those feelings sends a most important message, as the therapist tells a child that these feelings are not quite so scary and destructive, as much as they are actually parts of a child's inner world.

At this point, I was impressed by how Ethan was managing the stimulation of our play. Our sessions at this point were loud and a bit wild, as we sent our ships, with requisite sound effects, soaring around the room. Captain Pineapple was challenging, and it would have been easy and perhaps expected for Ethan to melt down at some point. Ethan also could have become annoyed by the similarities between my character and himself. After all, there is a presumption in creating a character that is designed to approximate another person. But Ethan stayed engaged and most of all calm, in a challenging albeit controlled play environment. Over the next two sessions, Ethan managed to foil the Captain's plans, as he successfully dumped the stolen supply of marshmallows by hitting the marshmallow ejector button, which Captain Pineapple had foolishly labeled and placed to the immediate left of the Earth Death Ray button. Ethan was quite pleased with himself, and I was pleased with his strength in stopping the intergalactic invader. Captain Pineapple had a brief tantrum before collecting himself and vowing his revenge. The Captain got frustrated but would not give up – I wanted him to hold on to his frustration without giving up hope for ultimate success. Captain Pineapple subsequently tried to rebuild his Earth Death Ray, but Ethan, who took great delight in defeating his new nemesis, once again vanquished him.

There was one problem.

Before our next session, I spoke with Ethan's mother who told me that in the past couple of weeks his progress had stalled. One day, Ethan got so angry that he locked his mother out of the house for several hours. While he had apparently been quite resourceful in figuring out how to trick her, that wasn't quite the therapeutic progress or creative energy I had in mind. At school, he was getting frustrated in class and was getting into arguments with other children.

I left the office wondering about Ethan's setback. Maybe Ethan had enjoyed an early therapeutic honeymoon phase and was now transitioning to a more realistic phase that would include ups and downs in his progress? Maybe he was trying to internalize our work and while doing so was struggling with his behavior? I wanted to believe this idea but it didn't feel right. Ethan wasn't all that subtle in how he operated, and his observable behavior seemed to reflect his emotional world. If he was struggling behaviorally, I knew he was also struggling internally. I thought about the other interventions he was receiving, wondering if there had been a change in his medication or in one of Ethan's other therapies. As much as I wished to fault somebody or something else, I needed to look at our work more closely, and the more I thought about it, the more I realized that whether I liked it or not, I was missing something.

I thought about Captain Pineapple. I had fully immersed myself in this character, thinking of new plotlines and twists that we could use in our sessions. I had imagined using Captain Pineapple to work on different challenges. I had planned to move from frustration tolerance and flexibility, to using Captain Pineapple in role-plays and simulated school situations. I imagined some of Captain Pineapple's fellow aliens landing on Earth, desperately in need of a guide to help them adjust to our planet. I had thought Ethan would be the perfect guide, and in the process his relationships with others would benefit. It all seemed so imaginative and helpful.

The more I thought about it, the more I realized that I had gotten ahead of myself, and most importantly too far ahead of Ethan. I had chosen to direct the play to prevent our work from becoming repetitive. Looking back over the last few sessions, I realized that our play was starting to resemble what I had been working so hard to avoid. There were longer pauses between Ethan and me, similar to the silences in a stale conversation, and Ethan's reactions were less varied, as his, and in truth my dialogue had become predictable. Our storylines centered on new ways that Captain Pineapple tried to conquer Earth, but they fell into a pattern that was becoming stale. The Captain would come up with a plan, subsequently make a mistake allowing Ethan to defeat him, and flee while vowing to return and conquer the planet.

Our early play had been warm and imaginative, because most of all, that play was based on the connection between Ethan and me. At our best, Ethan and I took turns, as when I pushed him to work with me on Lego, he allowed me in and then began to share with me his wealth of knowledge about space. At those moments, we were as dancers or actors, with one of us at times leading, but mostly we were working off of one another in a collaborative spirit. In my focus on storylines, junk food energy sources, and clever techniques, I had missed the point. In a way, I felt like an action film writer who has spent so much time on special effects that he loses perspective of the development of characters and their relationships. As the warmth of my exchanges with Ethan faded, so did the benefits of our work together.

In those earlier sessions, I was both an active participant and an active listener, paying attention to Ethan's emotional state and reflecting on my experience in the room with him at a given moment. I would notice his anxiety and frustration, which affected my reactions and informed my interventions. Ethan, in turn, picked up not only my words and my play but also the nuances of my tone of voice and body language that allowed us to engage nonverbally. I'd make a comforting comment, offer a reassuring glance, or place an arm on his shoulder to let Ethan know that I thought he was going to be ok. I hadn't done that since the emergence of Captain Pineapple. My reflections on the back and forth between us had waned, as in playing an intergalactic invader, I had stopped listening carefully to Ethan's, and my own, reactions and feelings, having gotten carried away with my own agenda. I was trying to do too much in this treatment. I was working very hard to try to keep Ethan connected and find a forum to work on his feelings. Too hard. In trying to push the therapy I was drifting further and further away from Ethan. Difficult as it was to admit, I was playing alone.

I had felt alone when I started working with Ethan, as he built his buildings and ignored me. In response, I took on an increasingly more assertive role in our work until ultimately feeling once again by myself. I needed to listen to this feeling, this aloneness which kept popping up in our work and which Ethan often struggled with in his life. More than anything else, I realized that I needed to change direction and slow down to find a way to reconnect with Ethan as the key to helping him.

We began our next session, and Ethan was ready to get started right away with Lego. I debated between re-engaging with him right away and addressing the family's difficulties at home. On the one hand, I was in the middle of working with Ethan and I was concerned that addressing his trouble at home would disrupt our work and that Ethan would respond to our conversation with the same series of monosyllabic responses he offered at the beginning of our work. On the other hand, I wanted to engage the family in the very difficulty that brought them into my office. They had begun, in that first session, with Ethan jumping around all over them. I wanted to return to the family challenges. I also made a bet that if Ethan had figured out how to commandeer the house, he might just be able to speak about the episode as well.

I told Ethan that we would play in a few minutes, but I wanted to speak with him and his parents first, as I had heard he had been getting very upset recently and I wanted to learn more about what was happening at home. Ethan wasn't thrilled, but with a little encouragement from me he sat down on a chair and we began talking. We talked about some incidents at home, including the one where he locked out his mother. We talked about how school was going and which kids he liked. We talked about what he could do to try to calm down when he was feeling upset and how he could begin to notice, whether from a feeling or a sensation in his body, when he was starting to become frustrated. Somewhere, in the middle of this conversation, we also talked about the moons of Jupiter and Saturn and of a visit to the Museum of Natural History. As Ethan reminded me again of the difference between Triton and Charon, we both smiled and reconnected. Then, we played with Lego.

ETHAN: (takes two of the little Lego guys). They're going into the building now.
ME: What are they going to do in there?
ETHAN: They're looking around. Not doing much.
ME: (I add a Lego guy to the group and talk for him, wanting to add a character while giving Ethan room in our play.) Hi guys, how's it going in here?
ETHAN: Oh, you know, it's great. We're having a great time.
ME: Cool. Mind if I hang out with you guys?
ETHAN: Sure!
ME: Fantastic. So, what are we going to do next?

ETHAN: Maybe we'll make some more buildings.

ME: Ok.

ETHAN: (Starts to work on a new building. Gives orders to the Lego guys to help). Hand over some red ones.

ME: Got it.

ETHAN: Blue and yellow ones.

ME: Ok. Anything else?

ETHAN: (Concentrating hard on the building, says nothing).

ME: (I clear my throat, but get no response. I do it again).

ETHAN: What?

ME: Anything else you need over there?

ETHAN: No, that's it. The building is finished.

ME: (I think of a way to keep our play moving as I sense Ethan is a little stuck) well, all that hard work has got me hungry.

ETHAN: Ok. Let's eat. Where do you want to go?

ME: Hmm, don't know. What do you think?

ETHAN: Maybe some hamburgers.

ME: Burgers are good. Now let's think of a great burger place.

ETHAN: McDonalds!

ME: I feel like going a little fancier.

ETHAN: Burger King?

ME: Same problem.

(We both think for a minute. I think about how we are building and how Ethan has enjoyed sharing his love of space with me).

ME: I have an idea. The Space Café!

ETHAN: (Looks interested and surprised) The Space Café? What's that?

ME: It's this new place. It's a restaurant, but everything is named after things in space, and the place looks like it's from outer space.

ETHAN: Terrific, let's go!

ME: (I get out of the character of my Lego guy and speak as myself). You know, we should probably make the café now.

ETHAN: But how?

ME: Let's get to work. What do you think we need? We're making a restaurant.

ETHAN: Food.

ME: (I start to write a list) Food, got it.

ETHAN: Tables.

ME: Tables got it.

ETHAN: Space decorations and dessert.

ME: Got those. How about menus?

ETHAN: Yes, we need menus. Write that down too.

ME: Ok, we've got food, tables, decorations, dessert; I'll put that under food, and menus. Shall we get to work?

ETHAN: Yeah, I'll build the tables and you write up the menus.

ME: I was kind of, you know, hoping, well, you'd do the menus with me.

ETHAN: Oh, ok. I'll do them with you. Let's go.

(Ethan and I get construction paper, markers and scissors and start making menus)

ME: It's time to write down what we're serving in this place!

ETHAN: Hmm. Burgers, fries, and hot dogs.

ME: Yes, of course. But, this is the Space Restaurant. We're supposed to have a space theme. Otherwise, we sound like we could be anywhere.

Ethan looked at me blankly. He didn't look angry or upset, he just didn't seem to know what to do. I wondered if I should give up here. After all, I didn't want to repeat my Captain Pineapple misadventures. But giving up the idea of nudging Ethan along would be a sorry result of my earlier missteps. So, I thought about a way to inspire Ethan without overwhelming him. I wanted to find a way to embrace his interest as a starting point and expand upon it.

ME: You know, something connected to space. Like a Mercury Milkshake or something like that.

ETHAN: Good we'll have Mercury Milkshakes. I'm writing that down.

ME: We'll need other stuff too.

ETHAN: (Thinks hard, smiles) Mars Meatballs!

ME: Terrific, what else?

ETHAN: Neptune Noodle Soup. Pluto Peanut Butter and Jelly Sandwiches.

ME: Not bad. And Charon Chicken Nuggets.

ETHAN: And Saturn Spaghetti!!!

ME: Yes, yes. Excellent!

We came up with and illustrated a fine intergalactic menu, featuring Earth Enchiladas, Venus Vegetable Stew, Meteor Macaroni, Comet Corn on the Cob, and Triton Tacos. The play was great fun for both of us, as we opened our restaurant to the public and entertained customers, played by various puppets, action figures, and Ethan's parents. Early in our play, Ethan had built beautiful, but empty buildings. Now, with my respecting and supporting his desire to build, and connecting it to his interest in space, Ethan and I had created a place bustling with the energy of hungry customers, busy waiters, and inventive chefs. My desire to connect to Ethan had been in the building all along; I just needed to listen more carefully, as the Space Café offered entry into the oft-hidden richness of Ethan's internal life.

At this point, summer was coming to a close and as planned, my work with Ethan started to wind down as he prepared to return to his regular school schedule. I met with Ethan and his parents for a few more sessions, so that I could make both play and practical family suggestions that they could continue to work on after we ended and so we could have a chance to say goodbye. We discussed a plan to transition to working with a therapist closer to their suburban home, who could continue some of our play-based work. Ethan's parents stayed in touch periodically over the next few months, updating me on Ethan's progress. He continued to move forward, managing the demands of the classroom and social arena while still struggling with the developmental challenges that remained with him. I wondered how our work would have evolved had we worked for a longer and more consistent period of time. My brief work with Ethan stimulated my thinking about how we develop a therapeutic space with a child. Active play nudged Ethan out of his comfort zone and helped me gain a foothold in Ethan's internal world. Actively introducing certain themes in our play also allowed us to engage with one another in a way that allowed Ethan to bring me in a bit further into his world, and in the process to develop an internal space within which he could start to work on his feelings and thoughts. But, our work wasn't successful when either of us was just tagging along. We both needed to be actively co-creating stories marked by a sense of warmth and invention. It was at those moments that Ethan showed his ability to become more flexible and more engaged.

My work with Ethan left me feeling that creating characters, such as Captain Pineapple or Pookie, has value and a particular place in working with children. Captain Pineapple has since made appearances in sessions with children who struggle with impulsivity as well as others who may be more timid and for whom Captain Pineapple offers a chance to voice a different part of themselves through the play. Sometimes he's a villain and sometimes a hero. Sometimes he's rather cunning, and sometimes he's a complete fool. Pookie, likewise, has been a therapy mainstay with a host of children including him in their stories as a goofy sidekick. And, most importantly, there are many children with whom I find no therapeutic value in adding these characters. Rather, with them, I may choose to follow their lead in developing the characters and themes that dominate our work (Kronengold, 2010).

There is an element of adventure to child therapy. The work is about following a path into a child's world, a path that can only be found by listening closely to a child's rhythms and experience. This listening is crucial as each child is different, calling for subtle changes in approach, often within a single session. I approached Ethan with an agenda of active play. I think that approach was helpful as long as I remained attuned to Ethan's rhythms and listened closely to my own reactions to make sure we were still traveling on a road together. When we lost our spirit of collaboration, our work stalled. On the other hand, when I listened to Ethan and allowed his interests to resonate with my own, the outcome was play that offered an emotional connection and growth.

I began this chapter with two well-known but enigmatic quotes from Winnicott and Axline, as I wondered about the role of a therapist's own play, imagination, and ideas in the work of therapy. I wondered how we develop a therapeutic space in our work. I still wonder. But, I think Axline's and Winnicott's statements belong together. I believe that our own creativity is crucial to our ability to work together with a child. It is this creativity that is emblematic of the healthy developmental energy that we wish for in therapy. Play will vary based on the personality and style of each individual therapist and also the particular chemistry between a therapist and a child. We may use metaphors, talk directly, draw pictures, or create characters. We may engage in play that can appear at turns intense, meandering, meaningful, and downright goofy. Sometimes we challenge, and sometimes we soothe. Sometimes we push forward, and sometimes we pause. We are constantly faced with decisions of how to proceed in the course of our work. Do we go right or left, forward or backward? Do we address a child's aggression or anxiety? Sadness or anger? Frustration or desperation? This is where our listening and our reflection are so vital, as we try to understand each child's emotional state and needs at a given moment. We listen, reflect, and try to sort out our own reactions, in the hope of being able to then engage and support a child. It is our very deference to a child's voice, our following a child's lead and willingness to meet his or her constantly changing emotional state, that allows us to enter into a child's world and help that child grow. It is our listening and respect for a child that offers us entry into his or her emotional world. Sometimes we follow a child's lead, and sometimes we play together. And, sometimes, maybe in the best of circumstances, we do both.

Permissions Acknowledgments

This chapter is copyright © 2012 by the Association for Play Therapy. Adapted with permission. The official citation that should be used in referencing this material is [Kronengold, H. (2012). The adventures of captain pineapple. *International Journal of Play Therapy*, 21(3), 167–185. doi:10.1037/a0028865]. The use of this information does not imply endorsement by the publisher.

4 Picturing a Frame

Sometimes I visit a school to observe a child or go to a meeting with teachers, parents, and other professionals. On occasion, I run into a child or family while I'm taking a walk, shopping, or riding the subway. At those times, I'll stop and say hello, maybe chat for a moment or two, and go on with my day. The work of therapy is meant for the office. It is that unique and boundaried therapeutic relationship that allows the work to move forward, as a child and family are given a special place that is devoted to the more intimate details of their emotional world. But therapy has a life outside the office as well. Children wonder about my life when they're not seeing me. They may wonder where I live, whether I have children and am married, and if so, to whom? What do I do with my spare time? Where do I go on vacation and what's my favorite restaurant? In truth, such wondering is a two-way street. I think about the people I see even when they're not in my office. I wonder how they're doing, whether at school or at home. In summer, I may think about how a child is enjoying camp, a new foray into independence. Finally, after I stop seeing a child, different questions pop into my head. Is a child doing well in school? Enjoying success at college? Has she kept up the same interests? Does he have close friends? Has he fallen in love? Is she happy?

This sort of wondering in therapy is reflected in approaches that have emphasized the therapist's humanity in therapeutic work, described in terms such as "therapeutic presence," (Moustakas, 1997; Crenshaw & Kenney-Noziska, 2014), "holding environment," (Winnicott, 1965), or the "personal signature of the therapist," (Stern et al., 1998). In early child therapy papers, shared tea and snacks are alluded to but rarely explicated, hinting at another layer to the child–therapist relationship. Once upon a time, Freud treated people in his home and joined them for dinner after completing an analysis. Today we live in more professional times with clearly defined roles. Our work takes place in what we hope is a comfortable office, and as the practice of psychotherapy has matured, we have developed clear guidelines and expectations of how therapy is conducted. Whatever theoretical approach we follow, there is often a playbook, perhaps overt or unspoken, that we follow. The question is, what happens when our ideas of how we are to conduct therapy are in fact challenged and when our best laid plans, however reasonable, need to be reconsidered when working with a given family.

At those times, we may not be able to rely on a given model or manual that tells us what to do. It is easy to rely on clear-cut techniques and stances when reading the literature, but what happens when therapists grapple with the muddiness of real-life experience, personal feelings, and reactions that don't fit into a neat box of theory and technique? Often, it is our presence in a child or family's life that becomes crucial in our work.

Diana called and left me a message saying that she was looking for a therapist for her 11-year-old son and had gotten my number from a colleague. I returned the call and we set up an appointment. A single mother of two children, Diana came in for a consultation to talk about her son, Joseph. Many parents begin speaking to me with hesitation, worried that they will be judged and often having critiqued themselves rather harshly for whatever predicament they may find themselves in. It is not uncommon for me to find out more complicated family details and history well into therapy. Diana was extremely open about her life with Joseph. She told me about her own personal difficulties when she was pregnant with him, and Diana carried immense guilt about the impact of her struggles on Joseph's development. As a young child Joseph had been diagnosed with epilepsy and had suffered from seizures, which had abated with the help of medication. He also presented with a history of significant learning disabilities. Joseph couldn't read and his other academic skills were significantly below grade level. To make matters worse, he was highly resistant to help, as he made quick work of a series of well-meaning teachers, specialists, and therapists. While accomplishing very little at school, Joseph also had few friends, an alarming video game habit, and fought regularly with his mother. His frustration and her guilt made for a particularly combustible family dynamic. Joseph had a neuropsychological evaluation at a New York City hospital where Diana shared the same information she had with me in our consultation. There, in an extensive report, lay every detail of their lives, with emphasis placed on Joseph's stunted development and Diana's failings as a parent. I felt both sad and embarrassed reading this report. Sad for the history the family was trying to overcome and embarrassed by the judgmental and hostile tone of the report. The point of this report was never clear to me. Perhaps the writer felt that she was being honest and right in her assessment. But where was the empathy and where was the desire to actually be helpful? I also realized that in my annoyance, I could go too far in defending the family. After all, self-righteousness works both ways. My job was going to be to help move them, both Joseph and Diana, in a direction where Joseph could become more independent and more invested in his own growth. Joseph was jaded and skeptical but Diana never gave up. She kept hoping and believing that life could and would be different for her son and she was very convincing. Despite Joseph's complicated history and myriad symptoms, I felt confident in beginning treatment.

Before our first meeting, I imagined Joseph to be surly and brooding. Instead, in walked a very friendly boy who sat down, went to pick up a ball he noticed on the floor, and started playing catch with me as we began chatting. Strangely, for someone so dismissive of help, Joseph seemed genuinely happy to meet with me. As our session came to a close, I told Joseph that we'd have to stop but that I hoped I'd see him again, as I always let a parent and child talk after an initial session about whether they wish to continue. Joseph looked at me like I was a fool, a look that would become very familiar to me over time. "Yeah," he said, "I'll be here, are you going anywhere?" "Ok," I said and laughed, "No, I'll be here. We do have to stop now though. I'll talk to your mom and we'll figure out our schedule." I walked Joseph out of my office and he walked over to his mom, and as they hugged each other, he looked back at me, beaming. I smiled back, a bit confused, as I started to realize that this had clearly not been an ordinary first session. Joseph and his mom (they existed together in my mind) were experiencing something that was clearly powerful but unknown to me. They looked so happy after that initial appointment. I must admit that I shared in their joy, excited at the beginning of what I hoped to be a helpful therapy, and a part of a more hopeful journey in their lives. But I was also wary. Had initial appointments with other therapists and specialists started the same way? What sort of fantasy was behind this excitement? Joseph and his mother had just met me. Clearly they were imbuing our beginning with something else – a longing for change and to find a person to help them. Their excitement was so strong and palpable, I worried about what would happen, as I suspected that the reality of working with me would likely pale relative to the fantasy of what I would help them accomplish. Then what?

The honeymoon continued over the first several months of therapy. Joseph came to our appointments enthusiastically, talked and played comfortably, and had begun to feel better about himself. He took greater care of himself physically, argued less with his mom, and appeared in a brighter mood in general. His mom was grateful for the therapy and was appropriately involved in wondering what she could do to help her son, while giving him room in his own therapy to do his own work. We had developed a nice rhythm in our sessions, as Joseph and I would joke, play some cards or catch, and he'd tell me a funny but bittersweet story about a dim-witted teacher or a kid on the bus. His learning difficulties concerned me, but I also knew that Joseph was extremely sensitive and ashamed about not being able to read. So, I chose to wonder with him how it was that someone so clearly very bright and curious, seemingly open to new insights and adventures, seemed so closed to the idea that his teachers could help him. I noted that he had similar feelings about therapists as well and seemed to be giving me a chance for the moment. I wondered aloud if he had started to give up prematurely, so that maybe he wouldn't have to feel bad about the whole annoying reading thing. I tried to wonder in a way that elicited Joseph's curiosity rather than embarrassment. While he didn't delve too deeply into my questions, he also didn't shut me down or ignore me, so I felt that we were planting the seeds for a deeper discussion at a later point. My wondering wasn't just for

Joseph, but for myself as well. In my office, Joseph was bright and animated, while the Joseph described in school reports was disengaged and utterly lacking in vitality. His teachers weren't surprised by Joseph's lack of achievement, just his mom, and now me. I wondered how that could be. Clearly Joseph felt understood and supported with me, and that helped bring out his healthier side. But in the process, was I missing an important part of him that I would need to access to be truly helpful? I started to wonder some more – it's easy to blame a teacher for not reaching a child, but how and why did Joseph take part in this dance?

As I wondered, Joseph and I kept working. Parents usually mail me payment but sometimes they prefer to hand it to me directly and so, Diana handed me a check after my afternoon appointment with Joseph. There are differences between handling payment face to face as opposed to the safer distance of mail but nothing significant had ever come up overtly before with a child in therapy. Not yet at least. As Joseph's mom handed me a check, Joseph called out to her, "What's that?" Diana casually responded, "It's for Dr. Kronengold." Joseph's face transformed, his eyes widening and mouth agape in surprise. "Wait," he said, "that's a check. Wait a minute. Wait! You get paid to do this! You get paid to hang out with me?" Joseph's reaction took me by surprise, and while no one else was in the waiting area, I felt constricted, aware I was in my waiting area discussing a personal matter, and fumbled for words. "Yes, I do," I muttered. "Remember, I mentioned that I talk and I play with kids, that's my job." Joseph looked back at me, annoyed. "I don't get it. Wait, how much do you get anyway?" as he waved his hand in the check's direction. I told Joseph that we could talk some more about it when I would see him next week and that I realized it was surprising to find out about the check. Still annoyed, Joseph agreed, we said goodbye, and my mind immediately began to fast forward as I wondered how I was going to handle this situation. I took a seat back in my office and took some notes as I kept flashing to the look on Joseph's face when he saw his mother hand me the check. It was in such contrast to his happy expression after our initial appointment. This wasn't just a look of surprise or annoyance. Kids regularly get angry at me and we deal with it. But, this look was different. I remembered the happiness on Joseph's face after our first sessions and realized I had now seen its distant cousin. I understood that Joseph felt betrayed.

In free moments that day, I replayed that awkward and painful moment after our session. I couldn't find the words at that moment, but what would have been the best thing for me to say or do? Should I have spent more time with Joseph talking about his reaction? But what would I have said? Should I have invited him back into my office for a few moments to speak? Perhaps he would have been able to leave our session feeling better. Then again, sessions often end on a difficult moment. As I sat there, worried, I started to rethink my whole payment policy. Maybe I should have a rule telling parents not to pay me in front of their children? But why not? After all, I care about the children I see in therapy, but it is also my profession. Why should there be shame in that fact? In any event, a policy wasn't going to help me very much at this point anyway. I was going to have to deal with my own anxiety now and wait until our next appointment. At that point I would see how Joseph was feeling, and talk with him about his disappointment. Who knows, I wondered, maybe a week's time would allow Joseph to cool off. Maybe this would be an opportunity, a chance for Joseph and I to discuss why he was upset and how this disappointment probably came up with other people in his life. Maybe we could discuss his father, absent from Joseph's life, and how Joseph wished for a male figure in his life. Maybe this difficulty with the check would allow us to deepen our work as we said goodbye to the honeymoon phase of therapy. Perhaps this check incident would, in the long run, be for the best? Or, perhaps not.

Joseph arrived at our next session on time and quietly walked into my office as if nothing was bothering him. He sat down and looked at me, as I considered whether to introduce the check incident at the start of our session. I decided to wait. I felt I needed to give Joseph some room and not respond so quickly to my own discomfort. I felt that it would be more therapeutic if Joseph could talk about his own feelings without my imposing them. I also realized that I might just be prolonging the inevitable and in the process allying myself with Joseph's desire to avoid this conversation. As Joseph gripped a foam rubber ball from my office, he talked about school and his latest video. The content of what we talked about was much the same as any other session but the emotion, the engagement, and the body language were all different; our session flat, our conversation distant. Joseph had cut himself off from his feelings or at the very least, from me, as he talked from afar. I allowed a few more minutes of conversation to see if we could warm up but to no avail. So, I decided it was time to bring up the check. Taking advantage of a pause in our conversation, I looked over at Joseph who was looking up at the ceiling.

"So I get paid." "Yeah," he said, with an exaggerated gesture. "You were surprised." There was silence. "You thought I met you without getting paid," I continued. "What does it mean that I do. Get paid?" "Nothing, it's your job," Joseph deadpanned as he continued to look away. "That's true. It's complicated. I mean, I like what I do. I like meeting with you." I looked at Joseph hoping to make some eye contact. "It's also my job and how I make a living. I get paid." But Joseph's gaze and voice remained distant as he responded, "You're repeating yourself now." I realized Joseph was technically correct and tried to use myself as a means to help us deal with the tension of the session. "Maybe it's because I'm uncomfortable." I paused. "Maybe you are too. You wish I met with you just because I just liked to. No other reason." Silence.

The only sounds for the next few minutes were the whooshing and clapping of an oversized soft rubber ball flying back and forth in my office. It started as a seemingly innocent game of catch, as Joseph tossed me the ball and I tossed it back. The sound of the ball grew louder as Joseph, his face taut and angry, began to take aim. I managed to catch the first few throws but the next sounds were of a ball hitting my hands and bouncing away as a game of catch evolved into a lopsided game of dodge ball. I jumped, twisted, and deflected as Joseph fired away.

"Maybe we should talk about this," I asked, as a ball zipped by my head. Silence. "I can see you're upset," I commented, as another hit bounced off my chest. Silence. "You know I actually could get hurt this way." Silence. "Maybe that's what you want right now." Silence. "I wish you hadn't seen the check." Silence. "I know you're disappointed. I really do like our time together. Even right now, well sort of, I mean, ok, we've had better moments. Still, I like seeing you and I want to keep seeing you." Silence. "If I told you I wasn't going to be paid, would that change how you feel?" Silence. "I'm running out of things to say. I wonder what would help." Silence. "I wish I could find the right words."

Finally, I stopped talking. I wasn't sure what to say anymore and had grown tired and frustrated dodging this ridiculous ball. Part of me wanted to keep coming up with things to say, hoping that at some point I'd at least stumble on some comment, observation, or question that could help get us out of this mess. But, I wasn't getting anywhere and the more I pressed the less helpful I became. As our appointment came to an end, I was afraid to end the session, worried that Joseph wouldn't come back. Maybe I should keep trying a little longer? Probably not. I suspected that would be more for my own needs than for Joseph's. I told Joseph that it was time to stop. He walked to the door and closed it behind without even a glance back at me. I wondered if he would come back to our next session.

A week later, Joseph sat in my waiting area, gave me a brusque "Hey," and a nod as we he got up to walk into the office. We continued therapy for another two months. At first, Joseph kept quiet but over the next month, as we muddled through, he started to talk about his life again. He became more engaged again with me in our conversations, but he also maintained a certain distance. His comments had a self-conscious quality, and he received mine warily. I tried to talk about how he might have felt but to little use. Our relationship had shifted since the check incident. While I was glad our work hadn't been completely derailed, the tone of our relationship had changed.

Joseph believed in me and in my relationship with him. He believed that I was meeting with him because I enjoyed spending time together and enjoyed trying to help him. He was absolutely right that I did enjoy those things. I also met with him as being a psychologist is my chosen profession, and I charge people for trying to help them with their challenges. There is a contradiction to this role as therapy is a helping experience involving both emotional intimacy and a fee for service. It's not an easy balance for a therapist, let alone for a struggling 11-year-old boy. To Joseph, I had ceased caring about him or enjoying our time. Rather, I had become hired help and my payment an act of betrayal.

At this point I wish I could write that Joseph and I worked through what had happened between us and resolved our impasse. That we had thoroughly come to understand why he felt so betrayed and in so doing, his relationships with others had become more realistic. I wish I could write that Joseph learned to trust me again and see that I could be a professional yet still care and want to help him. In fact, therapy didn't recover and after a couple of months of continuing, Joseph began to refuse to attend sessions. Diana and I spoke about continuing but she didn't want to push him too much. We agreed that Diana would stay in touch, she'd call me if something new arose, and we'd let Joseph cool off for a while.

While Joseph and I stopped meeting, he and his mom remained a presence in my office. Diana would call occasionally with updates, some good and some not so good, regarding Joseph's progress. He had definitely come out of his more depressed state from when I had first seen him, but he was still doing poorly at school. He wasn't learning much, didn't get along with teachers, and appeared unmotivated. He still couldn't read and Diana was advised by some professionals that maybe she would need to give up that dream. It's strange to call learning how to read a dream for a child growing up in New York City in the twenty-first century. It's particularly strange when that child is in a school setting dedicated to helping children with learning disabilities. But Joseph wasn't learning and he had been through so many teachers and specialists. The people who spoke to Diana were certainly empathic but wanted her to begin to accept a certain reality of Joseph's situation. Diana listened, cried for a while, and then did what she always did – looked for alternatives.

Diana called me with an idea that she admitted might be ill advised. She was thinking of homeschooling Joseph. Diana reassured me that she wasn't planning on doing the teaching herself. Rather, that Joseph would stop attending his specialized school, work with a tutor dedicated to developing reading skills, and in the process would also spend more time at home than in the past several years. Diana was increasingly frustrated at Joseph's lack of academic progress and felt that he wasn't advancing, nor was likely to advance, at his current school. What did I think?

Some years earlier I had been in a similar situation with a family who had a child who was struggling with various demands at school. The family had considered homeschooling, given the child's difficulties, and asked my opinion. I advised against the plan, as the child wouldn't have the same social opportunities and I thought his relationship with his parents would become too involved and unhealthy. The family chose to ignore my advice and went ahead with the homeschooling option. The boy in question enjoyed a very successful year of homeschooling during which time he became more settled emotionally and reengaged academically. He returned to school and over a decade later is enjoying life in college. Fortunately they ignored my advice.

With that learning experience in mind, I thought about Diana's options. I was worried that Joseph would miss out on social experiences, resist his mother's rules, and that the two of them would constantly be in each other's faces. Diana would also risk losing Joseph's Board of Education placement. If he left his current school and the homeschooling option failed, there would be few other options for Joseph in the future, other than a large classroom with insufficient resources. The negative possibilities were clear and worrisome. On the other hand, the current situation was hardly a successful one. Joseph was failing, and his mother was being asked to accept a future envisaging some vocational training and lifelong illiteracy.

Then there was the question of my role in this decision. I don't like to tell people what to do nor do I think it's the therapist's place to do so. Our job is to help people make decisions, rather than to make the decisions for them. It is by helping a parent come to a conclusion that we enable him or her to be able to make thoughtful parenting decisions as they move forward in life. Helping, though, means actively engaging a parent in the back and forth of their decision-making and working with them to consider the pros, cons, and intangibles that inform their choice. In this case, I admit that I imagined a greater future for Joseph. One may say that I was siding too much with Diana's notion of what he could accomplish while ignoring teacher and testing reports as to his limitations. But what if that's what Joseph needed – someone outside of his home who could imagine a brighter future than his history could conceive?

At the time, I thought of the work of Hans Loewald, who offered that it is the therapist's idea of who a person can be, as opposed to who that person may be at a current moment in time, that is often the most effective aspect of therapy. As Loewald said,

> If the analyst keeps his central focus on this emerging core he avoids moulding the patient in the analyst's own image or imposing on the patient his own concept of what the patient should become. It requires an objectivity and neutrality the essence of which is love and respect for the individual and for individual development.
>
> The parent–child relationship can serve as a model here. The parent ideally is in an empathic relationship of understanding the child's particular stage in development, yet ahead in his vision of the child's future and mediating this vision to the child in his dealing with him. This vision, informed by the parent's own experience and knowledge of growth and future, is, ideally, a more articulate and more integrated version of the core of being which the child presents to the parent. This 'more' that the parent sees and knows, he mediates to the child so that the child in identification with it can grow. The child, by internalizing aspects of the parent, also internalizes the parent's image of the child – an image which is mediated to the child in the thousand different ways of being handled, bodily and emotionally.

(Loewald, 1960)

I told Diana I thought her plan was a viable one, as long as Joseph came back to see me, or another therapist, at least periodically and that she was getting support with the dynamics at home. Diana had culled a variety of professional opinions and not surprisingly, there was discord amongst us. I completely understood the other position, and to be honest, I was worried when I advised Diana, as I knew that once she got some affirmation, she would go ahead with her plan. She knew what she thought was best; she just wanted someone to say it was Kosher, which was where I came in. So, Joseph began homeschooling.

Not surprisingly, with so many years of failure behind him, Joseph tested out his homeschooling teacher and brought a jaded attitude to his work. At Diana's request, I spoke with the teacher to fill her in on Joseph and she seemed understanding and patient with him. She also found Joseph exasperating but that was par for the course and I was delighted with her positive attitude. Despite some efforts, I had yet to see Joseph, though, as he embarked on this new schooling venture.

I left the office one evening and hopped on a bus headed home. As I took my seat, I heard a familiar "Dr. Kronengold," ring out from behind me. It was Diana, who was headed over to talk to me for a couple of minutes. Usually I just say hello for a moment or two but nothing about this case was typical. Diana talked with me for a few minutes about Joseph and then followed up our conversation a few days later with a call for Joseph to schedule an appointment to see me in therapy. It had been close to a year since our work together had ended. This time I walked out to the waiting room and saw Joseph and Diana sitting on a small bench outside my office. Diana smiled nervously, as Joseph looked quizzically and made his entrance. We sat down, looked at each other, and smiled. "Hello," Joseph said, with a wry smile. "And hello to you," I replied, eyebrows glancing upward. "So, it's been awhile," I added. "How are you?" Joseph nodded his head in his exaggerated way. "Ok, ok, I'm ok." "That's three oks," I noted. "And you are observant as always. Nothing gets by you," Joseph laughed. "I am a professional. It's all in the training you see." "Really, you worked on that." "Yes, we had a class, we'd have to count the number of times people said certain things. I was always really very good at it." "You were?" "Top of the class." "Sort of like a jellybean counting contest." "Well, yes, kind of," and we both laughed. As we laughed, a tension that had grown and calcified finally began to melt away. After a couple more jokes I finally said, "You know, it's good to see you and I'm glad you're back. You were pretty pissed at me last year." "Yeah, I'm over that." "I'm glad. (I paused.) It all started with that check." "Oh, yeah, I forgot about that." "Did you? Just kind of slipped your mind there?" "Yeah, ok, ok. I get it. We don't have to spend the next year talking about this you know. Let's not get too dramatic, ok," as Joseph jokingly put his hands up as if to calm me down. "Ok," I continued, "let me just say one thing. I do like you and I care about what happens to you. I do enjoy our sessions together and meeting with you. I'm just saying, I'm glad you're back."

I paused for a moment before I continued, as I wanted to address the rift from a year ago. "It's also true I get paid when I see you. I hope that doesn't have to ruin the rest of what I said." Joseph waves his hand, "Aah, it's ok." "You sure?" "Yeah." "Positive?" "Absolutely." "You're not going to throw stuff at me again?" I said, adding a little humor that I knew relaxed both of us and would open the door if Joseph wanted to discuss the issue further. "Not yet," Joseph added with that bemused smile and look in his eye.

So Joseph and I resumed. He needed time and the opportunity to take in and digest what had happened between us. I would have liked for Joseph to work through his residual upset from when we had been meeting a year earlier. But while working through can be encouraged and even nudged, it cannot be forced. A child needs to feel that there is a safety and a sense of control in order to be ready to explore his or her feelings, particularly when they are as deeply rooted as the ones that Joseph felt in our first sessions. I had to respect his pace and trust that even as he walked away for a time, he could still come back and deal with the feelings that needed addressing. In later sessions Joseph and I would again talk about the check, my getting paid, and his surprise and disappointment. It wasn't that our discussions were particularly groundbreaking but they gave Joseph the opportunity to deal with his feelings, and in the process, digest his sense of disappointment and betrayal. Over those next several months, Joseph and I worked together as he began the homeschooling plan. He insulted me daily, cheated on most card games, gave me his typically comical hard time, and seeing him again was an absolute pleasure. The color had returned to our sessions.

As for the rest of his life, Joseph began his homeschooling regimen, with an outside tutoring service managing his curriculum, much the way he had ended his formal school placement. The head of his tutoring group and I spoke from time to time, as Joseph gave his tutor a hard time, alternating between feigned indifference and outright hostility. I encouraged her to stick with Joseph, who if nothing else, could really use more people who believed in him. His antics were for show, hiding a vulnerability and a yearning that, if allowed to surface, could take Joseph farther than he had yet shown. As time went by, Joseph kept giving his tutor a hard time, changing the conversation, belittling a particular reading strategy, and insulting her personal habits and fashion choices. He also started to read.

For the first time in his life, Joseph was making academic progress. The work with his tutor was paying off, and his attitude to schoolwork was slowly changing from truculent to engaged. Joseph was able to turn his natural curiosity, humor, and intelligence to his schoolwork. He still struggled with his work. It was not as if Joseph had now become a fluid reader who was advancing at grade level. His learning challenges would realistically remain throughout his life. But, he was reading, doing his schoolwork, and learning more in the course of six months than he had his entire school life.

After several more months, Joseph and his mother decided that it was time for him to return to school. He had spent over a year in his homeschooling program and while his academic development was wonderful, Joseph wanted to be back with other kids in a classroom. As a result of his progress, Joseph gained admission to a stronger school that specialized in working with kids with learning disabilities. He was accepted for the next semester and in the meanwhile was enjoying his life. Joseph also made a decision that he wanted to stop therapy for at least awhile. He felt he was doing well, had made progress, and wanted to be more independent. I respected Joseph's decision, and in the spring we said goodbye again, with the plan that he and his mom would stay in touch. Over that spring, I heard a few times from Diana. His work had continued to improve to the point where people couldn't recognize him anymore as a student. Diana and Joseph fought at home but not more than other parents with their teenage kids. Joseph had turned a corner, and between his hard work and his mom's advocacy, he had gone farther over the past two years than anyone could have imagined. The last I had heard was that he was going to relax over the summer, and do some work with his reading teacher to keep sharp in preparation for the fall. After close to two years, Joseph readied himself to re-enter the classroom.

Joseph's new school was designed for students who had a mix of learning and developmental challenges. It was a different population from his previous school, which catered to children with more profound developmental vulnerabilities. I expected that the transition back might prove challenging and suggested that Joseph may want to meet before school started. But Joseph declined, preferring to go it alone. I was concerned about how Joseph would handle the workload, manage his return to learning in a large classroom, and integrate himself socially in his new school.

Over a week into school I received a message from Diana. Joseph had yet to attend a single day of classes. He was spending all day in bed, and despite Diana's best efforts, she couldn't rouse him. She worried that the school, which had been supportive thus far, would start to lose patience and Joseph would lose his spot as a student. Diana and I spoke, her voice cracking with trepidation over Joseph's state. She had never seen him this way, so depressed and lifeless. We made an appointment for Joseph to come and see me the next day. I wasn't sure he'd be able to get to my office and figured I might have to make more than one appointment. But, that morning, I buzzed Joseph in and came to greet him in the waiting room. He looked worse for wear. He sat on a chair, head hanging, eyes dropping, with his shirt out and his low hanging jeans looking more ragged than stylish. He also greeted me with a knowing and sharp look that reassured that despite this difficulty, the resilient Joseph was still there and ready to be re-engaged. Joseph sat down in the office, looked at me again, and started – "Hey." "Hey, you look a little, well, I'm trying to think of the right word." "Tired?" "Maybe a little more." "Very tired?" "Not quite." "Ok, strung out?" At this I knew our usual humor was still going to work and decided to continue. "Getting there," I said. "Homeless?" Joseph wondered, with a wry smile starting to meander its way. "Too judgemental," I noted. "Never mind, you get the idea," I said. "You look kind of, well, let's be honest, terrible. What's going on? I heard you can't get out of bed?" "Yeah." At this point our banter ended and Joseph and I moved into a more serious discussion. The twinkle in both our eyes was replaced by seriousness and we both understood he was going through an immensely challenging and profound moment in his young life. We meandered in our conversation, wondering about his school anxiety and the details of trying to get to the bus in the morning. After a pause, Joseph looked at me again, paused once more, and finally blurted out, "I, I, I just don't know if I want the responsibility."

I remember Joseph's honest words, spoken years ago, as if it were yesterday. He was so clear in that moment. Joseph understood how much his life could change with going back to school. He would be on a course which would lead him through high school and give him the chance to attend some sort of college and get a degree. Before that, he had been on track to need ongoing help with limited vocational training as his best option. When we had first met, Joseph needed support in so many areas of his life. He needed help in school and at home. He couldn't stop playing computer games and struggled to take care of his physical needs. He had come so far. In the process, he had become frightened, not sure if he could handle this new world he was venturing toward. Instead, he stayed in bed. It's a feeling we can all relate to from time to time. But for Joseph, the feeling had spun out of control, leading him to a darker and debilitating depressive episode that was threatening all his hard fought work. Joseph's honest words were stark and upsetting but his honesty led me to believe that he would be able to move forward.

Joseph's school principal was very sympathetic to his struggle and was committed to helping Joseph. School allowed him to start off on a modified schedule, with Joseph attending classes for just part of the day if he needed. His mother was willing to provide transportation so Joseph could attend at least part-time. Joseph's father had made an entry back into his life and had volunteered to help as well. Slowly, with support, Joseph began to get out of bed and made his way to school. At first just part of the day, but soon, Joseph was getting acclimated and making friends. Within a few weeks, he was back to school, arriving punctually to the bus stop every morning and resuming the success that had seemed so uncertain just a month earlier.

I finished the rest of the academic year seeing Joseph in therapy and speaking with his mother to make sure things were ok at home. As we wound down for the summer, Joseph was in good spirits and had received a very solid report card. He was getting busier socially, and he and I agreed that he take a break from therapy and check in occasionally to see how things were going. Knowing that the return to school in the fall could be challenging, we also agreed to meet in September just to make sure things were going smoothly.

I saw Joseph that fall for a couple of sessions and his transition issues appeared behind him. We agreed that he or his mother would call to keep me periodically updated. In the early winter Diana left me a message to let me know how well Joseph was doing in school and to catch me up on some remaining home conflicts. An occasional follow-up call came in to ask me about a particular question or a summer plan. At that point, Joseph's life appeared back on course and I took my typical role as a child's therapist following therapy. I was there to help if called upon, but I really didn't expect more than a periodic check-in.

This next call occurred in Joseph's junior year in high school and was wonderfully unexpected. Diana contacted me to let me know that Joseph needed a brief testing done so that he could qualify for both extra time on standardized testing and learning resources at his next school. Joseph was going to apply to a two-year college program with the hope of then transferring to complete a full four-year undergraduate degree. He had asked if I could do the assessment with him. Normally I don't assess kids who I see in therapy. The two really don't mix very well. Therapy has an open-ended feeling and is based primarily on a relationship between a child and therapist. Testing on the other hand involves asking a child to complete a variety of cognitive and academic tasks. It is best done when an evaluator can easily administer standardized tasks without too much emotional baggage carried along the way. I've tested kids whom I have seen in therapy a couple of times because of a particular financial or therapeutic reason and had always regretted the decision. The child, accustomed to working with me in an open-ended fashion, bristled when I suddenly was asking vocabulary questions and timing their responses on certain items. The kids I had tested also felt more self-conscious with me, worried that my image of them had diminished because they made a mistake on a visual–spatial task or a reading comprehension question. Therapy is supposed to be accepting. Testing is supposed to be accepting as well, except when it isn't, which is probably why it's called testing.

Based on my previous experiences, I hesitated with Joseph's request. The last thing I wanted Joseph to feel in our work was a sense of failure. On the other hand, I hadn't seen him in therapy in a couple of years, the assessment would be brief, and Joseph had specifically asked for me to do this evaluation. I respected that Joseph might have a reason to do so. In truth, I also wanted to be the one who did this assessment. I had been through so much with Joseph. I admired his strength and his mother's resilience. I had wondered about him frequently when we had stopped therapy, and now that he was going to college, this boy who couldn't read a few years ago, well, I wanted in my own way to be part of that. Was that wrong? Was it narcissistic of me to want to feel part of his college process? Maybe. But what if in this case, I was part of that process, and part of the large extended therapeutic and support family that Diana and Joseph had developed over the years?

Joseph walked into my office and greeted me with a familiar smile. He was taller than me now, with a couple of days' worth of stubble on his chin, and a confidence to his gait. "It's good to see you," I said. "Yeah, you too. It's strange to be back." "I can imagine. Different circumstances though, right." "I know, I'm going to go to college. Crazy, huh?" "Your mom made my day when she left me that message. How are you feeling these days?" "I'm going to college. You know. So pretty good. Just crazy you know, right?" "I know, who would've thought a few years ago, huh? Imagine if someone had told us when we started, when you were little, that we'd be meeting again to do this thing so you can get extra time on the SATs?" "I couldn't read or spell the word then. Yeah (hand gestures)." "Yeah (I gesture myself)." With that greeting, Joseph and I began the funniest assessment I've ever done. I read lists of numbers for Joseph to repeat and at the point at which he couldn't remember he just started making up strings of nonsense numbers and syllables, all with a self-deprecating laugh and usual eye roll. The more difficult vocabulary words offered more room – "What's that word? Wait, you mean that's an actual word? It is English, right? I just learned how to read a couple of years ago. I don't think you should be asking me a word like that. I mean, you know, I could start to feel really bad and then, you know, it's over." "Just like that?" "Just like that, I'll give up. I'll be right back in bed." Then there was Joseph's deconstruction of other questions. "So, Ana drove 20 miles in her car. Joe drove 10 miles and Rob drove 15 miles. How many more miles did Ana drive then Rob?" "Wait. What happened to Joe? Why isn't he in the question when he was in the story? It's like they just threw him in there (he adds with emphasis) to confuse you. Man! (He throws up his hands exaggeratedly)." Finally we got to the arithmetic question of a little boy named Miguel. "It was Miguel's eighth birthday. His mother gave him (I pause for a second) a dollar." "Poor kid." I bite my lip trying not to laugh as I continue the question. "Miguel bought a pen for 19 cents." "This is depressing." "And, (at this point I really can't stop from starting to laugh) a comb for 26 cents." At this point Joseph is laughing loudly, I'm cracking up, and he looks at me. "How much does this test cost?" "You don't want to know." "Yes I do, this is terrible. I mean, I feel awful right now. For Miguel. I don't even know the kid. He doesn't even exist and now I'm in a bad mood."

Our two sessions went on like this. A bunch of questions and tasks, some very funny, shared moments, a brief report for school and college applications. Most of all, Joseph and I were just enjoying ourselves. After all he'd been through – the epilepsy, school problems, depression. After the rupture in our relationship, here he was, sitting with me taking a bunch of tests designed to help him move to the next stage of his life. Most of my time with kids is spent trying to help them when they're struggling. Once they're feeling better they usually leave and I don't have much contact with them or their families anymore. The chance to meet with Joseph felt like our own celebration. We wished each other well, I confirmed with his mom that the report had covered what she needed for college, and Joseph went on his way to start his applications.

From time to time I wondered about Joseph. I hoped he was doing well and had kept up his grades to support his application. I wondered where he would go to college and what he would study. I wondered how he would feel away from home for the first time. Living with roommates. Having new experiences. I was excited for this next chapter in Joseph's life. Only it went terribly off course.

Several months later I received a terribly unexpected message from Diana. She was calling from the hospital. Joseph had been very sick for the past two weeks and after days of medical tests, had been diagnosed with an aggressive form of leukemia. Could I please call her back she asked, her voice straining for calm on my answering machine.

I sat in my seat numb for a moment. How could that possibly be true? How could a young man who had overcome so many challenges, who was about to make the most crucial of choices, and take advantage of new opportunities, fall ill? Epilepsy, dyslexia, leukemia. It couldn't be. He was too young for all this. It wasn't fair. It was like some sort of cruel joke. It was impossible.

I picked up the phone and reached Diana, who cried and then composed herself, as I did my best to stay calm on my end of the line. Diana mentioned that the doctors thought it could be a rare side effect from the epilepsy medication he had taken as a child. Joseph was trying to stay strong but very upset. He would be in the hospital on and off for treatment over the next several months with his first round having just begun. Could I have sessions with him in the hospital?

Psychotherapy is meant for an office, where there's a privacy and a safe therapeutic space that offers a chance to explore feelings that may not be as accessible in the regular world. Sometimes though, life doesn't fully cooperate, and my work with Joseph and his mom had always been on the unconventional side. When I walked into Joseph's hospital room I realized privacy might be an issue with the various medical personnel zipping in and out of his room. I also realized that that was the least of the problems facing the young man who had on his usual brave game face, as he sat in his hospital bed sparring with the head nurse, who had clearly tired of Joseph shortly after his arrival. We looked at each other and exchanged one of those looks again, the kind that captures a whole range of dialogue. A look that says this is completely screwed up. I'm so sorry you're here. Would you believe the kind of crap I've got to deal with now. I'm scared shitless. I get that. This is completely insane. All those unspoken words were expressed as we said hello to each other. I took a seat by his bedside as Joseph cursed at his nurse.

I don't really remember the back and forth discussion from that session at the hospital. I sat with Joseph, and we talked about the hospital, how he was feeling, and how he found out he was sick. He lay there in his hospital bed, surrounded by a tangle of intravenous tubes, vital sign wires, and video game connectors. Ever the gamer, Joseph had his Xbox game console next to his bed. As usual, he was matter of fact. Who could blame him? He was also feeling ill with a fever that had spiked earlier in the week following an unforeseen infection. Mostly, I just sat with Joseph and listened to him complain. He had a right to. I left after we were interrupted for the third time by a nurse who needed to check Joseph's vitals and administer medication. I headed down to the hospital lobby, spoke to Diana in the waiting room, headed out of the hospital and decided to take the twenty-minute walk back to my office as I wondered how I was going to help Joseph during this ordeal. Most of all I wondered if Joseph was going to make it.

I visited two weeks later. Joseph's infection had proved unresponsive to treatment, and he was weak and exhausted. Simple movements were more of an effort this time, as Joseph needed some help getting up in his bed and getting food from his hospital tray. Joseph didn't have much to say, or perhaps he didn't have the energy. He told me a little about his routine and the details of how sick he had been feeling. His friends from school had been in touch with him and Joseph pointed to the cards and presents they had sent him, his eyes perking up a bit as I read aloud some of their notes. Joseph's usual resilience was impressive as always. It would have been easy for him to sink back into his bed and give up at that point. At that moment, I realized that having people around helped support Joseph and my job was going to be to stick around, give him support, and be available for him to talk to me.

I needed to call ahead before seeing Joseph to make sure he was both available and up for meeting. On some days, a treatment, appointment, or test had been scheduled, while on others, Joseph had come back from a procedure and was too exhausted to meet. I kept in touch with Diana, who was spending most of her time at the hospital managing Joseph's treatment and on occasion I spoke briefly to Joseph on the phone.

When I next saw Joseph in-person, a month later, he was feeling stronger, studiously playing a video game, as I entered his room and sat down. It was hard for Joseph to pull himself away from the game, and as I took a seat, he barely acknowledged me and kept his eyes focused on the screen. We sat like this for the next few minutes before I tired of the routine and decided that Joseph was probably ready to resume our usual relationship. "Well, this is nice. I come all the way over from across town to visit you, here in the hospital, and you're sitting here playing with your little game. Very nice." Joseph chuckled for a second, put down the game, turned toward me, looked over and without missing a beat said, "I'm sorry, please tell me about your problems today. I'm in the hospital with leukemia. Please, go ahead." Taking my turn I continued – "Well, it began with the elevator in my office building. It was delayed." "How awful." "Then I had to wait for the bus and get this, I get on the bus, and there's no place to sit. I had to stand the entire time to get here today." "It's rough." "I know, I'm exhausted. Can I have a moment?" "Sure, take all the time you need." I pretend to catch my breath and equilibrium for a moment. "Ok, that's better. So anything happening in your life these days?" "Hmm, let me think for a second. Not much really. No. Well, wait. There's one thing. Oh, yeah. Cancer!"

I'll never know exactly how Joseph and I would get into these comic rhythms. Clearly, we both enjoyed using humor to cope. More importantly, we used humor as a means to connect and join together at those moments when words might fail. Or, at least when each of us failed to find words but managed the bittersweet absurdity that captured the fear of Joseph's situation. The humor reconnected us, and we talked about how much longer Joseph would stay in the hospital and his plans once he left. We imagined Joseph's college essays centered on childhood epilepsy, severe dyslexia, and leukemia. "I have the perfect application. Can you imagine someone saying no to me?" We cracked up imagining how he'd write this tragic essay and the possible conversations he'd have at interviews. How amazing to laugh when Joseph was hoping to stay alive.

Over the next couple of months, Joseph continued to improve. His treatment was working, and as I went to visit a month later, Joseph was looking better and in stronger spirit. He wasn't even fighting with the nurses much anymore and instead was focusing his attention on getting back to school. Consistent with Joseph's hopes, his medical tests were coming back clear and his leukemia was in remission. He knew that he would need to be monitored regularly for the next two years before he could be considered fully in remission but Joseph was feeling more hopeful as he returned to complete high school.

I made a follow-up call a few weeks later to check on Joseph. He had returned to school and seemed to be doing well, managing his classes, reconnecting with friends, and having standard teenage boy arguments with his mom. I checked in a couple more times, and Joseph was moving along. We left open the possibility of him coming to my office to meet, but for the moment, Joseph preferred to get back to his regular life as a high school senior. That was the last I heard from Diana or Joseph for the next several months.

The next time I heard Diana's voice on my answering machine, I tensed, as I knew that Joseph would be observed carefully for any resurgence of the leukemia and was worried about what Diana was about to say. I relaxed as Diana began to ask me for some supporting documents so that Joseph could attend a two-year college program. Needless to say I was delighted to hear this information, called Diana back and heard the good news directly that Joseph was once again progressing and healthy. I received periodic calls, as Joseph headed off to school, enjoyed success and reached his two-year milestone of staying leukemia free. He completed his Associates Degree and made plans to shift to another university to finish up his studies. What a journey Joseph had taken.

Of course Joseph's story doesn't end at this point. The natural ending point for this story would be Joseph's enrollment in full university and a happily ever after finish. But, the whole point of this therapy is that very little went according to form or plan. Rather, our work constantly shifted alongside the ever-changing challenges, opportunities, and twists of fate in Joseph's life. Working with Joseph has been the greatest lesson in the ebb and flow of therapy, and the unpredictable nature of what happens when two people work together within an intimate emotional space. As therapists, we can develop techniques, models, and frames, and we should continue to do so to further our work and our ability to help individuals who experience a certain distress. The human component of our work is always central though, and sometimes it takes a therapy such as working with Joseph to remind us, or at least one therapist, of the critical nature of our personal relationship with any person who engages with us in therapy and of our respect for that individual's unique and unpredictable path in life.

Walking not far from my apartment on a sunny fall weekend morning, I heard a familiar sounding "Dr. Kronengold," calling down the street. I walked over to Diana, asked her how she was doing and what was the latest news about Joseph. "Can he come and see you again?" "Of course," I said, looking at her in anticipation. Diana continued – "He's visiting from college and he's not happy. It's kind of been a mess recently. I think it would be good for him to talk to you and he said he'd like to see you." I told Diana that of course I'd be happy to see him, and so there, on the corner of Broadway, we made plans to resume the latest chapter in our work.

5 Real Madrid 18 – Tottenham Hotspur 18

"Welcome to the Bernabéu. It's a beautiful day today here in Madrid, as the home side, led by the great Cristiano Ronaldo and his all-star Real Madrid teammates, take on Tottenham Hotspur, featuring the new Footballing sensation, Gareth Bale. Madrid heavily favored here in this Champions League final, looking for yet another title. They meet a surprising Tottenham squad that has come out of nowhere to challenge the European greats. The world watches and wonders – will this be yet another victory for Madrid or, can Tottenham, the Cinderella squad, pull off an incredible upset? The stadium is packed with anxious fans. The anthems sung, they kick off and Madrid have the ball, looking to attack. Ronaldo dribbles forward. He protects the ball as he looks upward toward goal. Always searching, looking for that opening. Ronaldo cuts back with his right, back again with his left, leaves the Tottenham defense in shambles! He shoots! Oh, how close! Just inches wide! What an opening statement made by Real Madrid! How will Tottenham respond? You have to wonder how these players feel in what is the biggest game thus far in their careers! The ball comes to Tottenham star Gareth Bale who marches forward, looking to make a first impression of his own. Bale dribbles with pace down the side. Can Spurs possibly strike first!"

Not everyone likes to play with castles, puppets, or pretend animals. Not all children like to draw, use sand, or even play Lego. In fact, some children actively dislike or turn up their noses at such play, preferring instead to play sports, active games such as baseball, basketball, or soccer. Often, these kids are boys, though not exclusively so, as I've spent plenty of time playing different sorts of games with a wide variety of children. The point is that there are individual differences in a child therapy room, which impact what and how children play.

There are also differences amongst therapists. Frankel (1998) talks about his own preferences in play and their likely impact on the children he sees. For example, he mentions how children in his office tend toward a more active and dramatic play, using furniture as tents and roaring like angry lions, in contrast to a respected colleague of his whose sessions tend quieter and involve dolls, sand, and art. Bellinson (2002) talks about her use of board games in child therapy, while admirably admitting that physical ball play is an uncomfortable venue for her. A therapist comes to the child therapy room with his or her own personality, interests, and talents, not to mention history. How these interests and predilections match a child's may prove critical to the course of therapy.

The question is whether one type of play is better than another. Some types of play clearly lend themselves to symbolism and a rich forum for metaphor, while others can seem concrete. In the case of sports, we often talk about its positive impact on physical and social development and a resulting increase in self-esteem. We rarely talk about sports as a medium for deeper emotional or psychological experience.

But is that true? Of course physical exercise, mastery, and self-esteem are wonderful, but what about children for whom sports is more profoundly personal? What of children who experience the world through action and for whom ball playing occupies a psychologically meaningful space? The fact is that sports are a favorite activity for many children. It's why gym and recess, typical times for playing basketball, football, tag, and the like, are frequently the most popular times of a school day. It's why so many children love going to the park and why summer camp is so memorable. There is a freedom, a unique and often expressive experience that comes with physical activity. Jennings (1990, 2011) talks about the importance of embodied play in a child's development of identity, emphasizing the role of physical forms of play that may begin in infancy but continue to arise throughout childhood and adolescence. Her work, while inclusive of all forms of drama and role-playing, focuses on the place of physical experience, including movement and dance, as a critical and naturally expressive medium for children.

Alex was one of those kids who had no interest in my traditional imaginative play toys. He edged into my office tentatively, carefully looking around as he stood near the doorway while gazing backward to his mother in the waiting area. I invited Alex to look around, and as he quietly surveyed his surroundings, I introduced him to my castle and assorted knights, a playhouse with pretend animals, then over to some puppets, art supplies, and action figures. An unimpressed Alex kept walking, stepping carefully, his eyes warily taking in the art on my walls, placement of my chairs, and view from the window. I opened up the top of a large bamboo storage basket sitting at the edge of the area rug in the corner of the room, alerting Alex to the Lego inside. Still no interest. An athletically built eight-year-old, Alex carefully navigated around my office, avoiding a couple of small blocks left on the rug and the edge of a chair. He stepped softly, placing one foot in front of the other as if measuring the solidity of the floor underfoot. Alex happened upon a small vinyl covered squishy soccer ball. His eyes finally stopped and Alex held the ball in his hands, turning it from side to side. "Do you like soccer?" I wondered aloud. "Uh-huh," Alex replied, the nodding of his head resonating more loudly than his words as he rushed a quick and barely audible "do you?" in response. "Well, it so happens, yes." I paused for a second and after a silent moment added, "I kind of became a fan last year." Alex's head perked up with interest. "Who do you like?" he asked me. "Who?" I wondered. "Which team?" Alex explained. "Tottenham

Hotspur," I answered proudly, and Alex raised his eyebrows. "I like Real Madrid. Who's Tottenham?" he asked. "They play in England," I explained. Alex paused a moment, then he continued, "I know some teams in England, Chelsea, Manchester United. Do you ever play soccer?" I paused a second before answering, "yes, sometimes." "On a team?" Alex wondered. "No, for fun," I explained. "Ok," as Alex nodded his head again before continuing, "who do you play with?"

So began my soccer journey with Alex. His parents had recently divorced and Alex presented with difficulties principally related to anger and anxiety. Alex kept things inside, keeping his worries and frustrations to himself. Eventually, these feelings would get the better of him and Alex would either blow up or become exceedingly fearful, particularly at home with his mother and brother. The divorce had been difficult and Alex missed his father's presence.

"Do I like soccer?" Alex had asked. "Who do I like? Who do I play with?" A series of questions, for a child of few words, all starting with the discovery of a little squishy soccer ball and the mention of two foreign soccer teams. I do like soccer. In fact, it had become a bit of a thing for me, which hadn't always been the case. As a child I much preferred basketball and baseball and had little exposure to soccer. That would all change, as my own children began to play in our neighborhood recreational league and I transitioned into a soccer dad. My interest in the game continued to grow. I would join my kids and stop by our local soccer shop to look at the latest cleats with them and meander. The store has a large-screen TV, comfortable mini stadium seats, and broadcasts all the English Premier League games. Soon enough, I became a fan of a particular English squad, whose combination of stylish attacking play, Harry Potterish sounding name, and classic jerseys, proved irresistible. I became a fan of Tottenham Hotspur.

In most cases, this information would be completely irrelevant. Some might say that my history with soccer and choice of a random English squad actually is completely irrelevant and offers nothing to my work with children. Some may even opine that my own sharing of this interest is detrimental. It's a fair perspective that is shared by clinicians across various orientations, who recommend against the therapist muddying the waters with his or her own life and interests. I can understand this idea. Therapy is about finding entry into a particular child's world and creating a therapeutic space with which to explore it. Such a perspective doesn't require me to share the same interests, as much as to be open to a child's experience and to find a way to engage that child. In fact, my own interests can serve as a distraction, take away from the emphasis on a child's experience, and even create an unspoken expectation for a child to conform to my world rather than the other way around. The latter can be particularly ill-advised, as so many children who enter therapy already struggle with the difficult expectations of a world that can often feel mismatched to their temperament, reactions, or interests.

However, a therapist's personality and life will prove critical in a subtle or overt manner. It is for that reason that we talk of finding a right match between therapist and child, rather than the idea that all therapeutic relationships are somehow interchangeable. As if the meeting place to explore a child's world can be reduced to a formula or recipe from a cookbook. The work and the challenge though, is for the therapist to use his or her personality to facilitate the work of therapy. Alex was a huge soccer fan, and my own fandom offered entry into his world and a particular connection between us. Perhaps that would have occurred regardless of my interest, but I suspect not. I have always played sports in my office. It just so happens that since my soccer fascination began, I've played more soccer in a two-year period than I had in the previous twenty years of my training and clinical practice.

In Alex's case, our shared interest certainly helped him feel comfortable in sessions. He began to show up in a Real Madrid or Spanish National team jersey, often arriving at my office following his own soccer practice. In due time he added cleats and shin guards to the mix, as our sessions started to feel like a scrimmage. Alex entered my office, walked over to the soccer ball, said "ready?" or "can we play soccer?" and with my approval began to set up the makeshift goal areas that we designed using chairs, baskets, and garbage cans as posts. My vaguely rectangular area rug served as a modified soccer pitch. I looked to our playing as a means of expression for Alex. I expected that soccer would both help him feel comfortable in therapy and serve as its own form of dramatic play, with our games as developing narratives for his world.

We played. Alex would make his moves with the ball and I would guard him. I'd play with a measured seriousness. I wouldn't just let Alex dribble past me easily but I also didn't try too hard as I wanted him to have to work, but not excessively, to beat me. So I'd guard but with limited pressure and played at half speed when I had the ball. My soccer skills aren't particularly strong, so while I can perform the most basic of soccer moves, I didn't need to ease up that much when I was playing with Alex. We kept score but without much focus on the outcome, which ended easily in Alex's favor. After a few sessions, it was clear that Alex had grown comfortable in my office. I also began to feel constrained by our play. It was tentative and overly polite. It felt a bit more golf than soccer to me. I felt that I needed to move the play forward a bit. I wanted to make the game more exciting, more fun. More embodied. Alex was tentative in life while his emotional world simmered underground. I thought soccer could bring some of his unvoiced feelings to the surface.

I also wanted to respect Alex's playing style and not get too competitive. Alex was careful for a reason, so I decided to add a bit of effect by introducing an outside character in the same way I might in a traditionally imaginative form of play. I became a player/announcer: An announcer who could properly convey the excitement of the game rather than just bland commentary. It so happens I enjoy accents and find they lend a playful and emotional color to sessions. The simplest and most concrete game can become a playful and affective exercise with the right vocal turn. It's sort of like a soundtrack to a film, adding a layer of emotional color to the therapeutic space. So, I became a Scottish/Northern English accented announcer, who inspired by my own TV viewing, was prone to the melodramatic. The very accent, if one can imagine for a moment, conveyed a sense of the sport, which we now started to call football, as more than a game, but an endeavor full of heart and soul. To add, even saying "heart and soul" in a Scottish accent better expresses the depth of feeling involved. I found that the more Scottish I became, the more animated Alex became in our games, both enjoying the fun and playing with greater intensity. We were no longer just shooting around at this point or politely defending. Rather, Alex would start making moves and played tighter defense while I responded in kind. I wasn't sure what was going on at this point, but I knew that we had moved into a more emotionally resonant stage in our sessions.

During these games we spoke about Alex's beloved Real Madrid. Alex was a huge fan of the club and their star player, Cristiano Ronaldo, an immensely talented footballer who carried quite a chip on his shoulder. Ronaldo was always searching for recognition and furious at the adulation directed at his more popular nemesis Lio Messi, the star of arch rival Barcelona. Alex also loved Xabi Alonso, Real Madrid's soulful midfielder, and Iker Casillas, their fantastic and charismatic goalkeeper, who served as the more humble glue and tough spine of the club, beside the preening yet fantastically talented Ronaldo. It was hard for Alex to watch games. He loved the spectacle, but he would also get so upset if his team struggled. Real Madrid was an extension of himself, with the various players serving as alter egos to different parts of his personality. It is easy to look condescendingly at such vicarious defeats, unless one can relate to the connection a person can feel to a team and the genuine despair that comes when that team loses (Hornby, 2005; Kleimberg, 1998). It is helpful to remember that there is a reason why cities have parades for their championship teams and experience a collective mourning for their losing ones. Fortunately for Alex, only a select number of Spanish games were broadcast and Real Madrid usually won anyway, so he was spared too much frustration. Alex also knew I preferred Barcelona, but my choice was not much of an issue, as he knew that my real team was Tottenham.

"I'm going to be Madrid today, how about you?" Alex announced as he came into session.

This was new. "What team do you think I should choose?" I replied, pleased that Alex had suggested a more dramatic channel for our games. "I don't know," Alex shrugged, "you decide, it's your choice." "Well what do you think?" I reflected. "I don't know," Alex repeated, "whatever you want." "No suggestions?" I added. Alex shrugged with his hands, "Really, you choose." I was delaying as I thought for a moment about which way to go. Barcelona. Real Madrid's arch rivals, would be really intense. But, one team felt genuine. "I'll be Tottenham," I offered with the slightest bit of swagger, as Alex smiled and nodded approvingly.

Sports rarely feature in the child and play therapy literature. In a world that values the clearly symbolic, sports can be seen as active, concrete, perhaps even lowbrow and too aggressive for therapeutic work. That said, sports aren't completely ignored. Hudak (2000) talks about the importance of ball playing as a means to build rapport and therapeutic context. His ideas have been shared by countless therapists who help a child feel comfortable by playing ball and subsequently transition to therapeutic conversations or traditional play. Altman (1997) goes a step further as he considers sports as a therapeutic medium. He sets the scene of play in Madison Square Garden in the early 1990s, as he works with Ronald, a seven-year-old boy and massive New York Knicks basketball fan. Ronald takes on the role of his beloved Knicks while pitting Altman as his arch rivals. In his paper, Altman stresses the manner in which a therapist and child can enter a world of physical and competitive play, particularly sports, where personas are adopted, omnipotent fantasies enacted, and rivalrous and competitive feelings are given a forum for a young boy who had lacked such a space in his life. Altman and Ronald played hard, made crowd noises, argued with referees, and at times, even with each other. Altman's paper is basically a long answer to the question he poses at its end – "But isn't basketball a purely competitive physical activity lacking symbolic content?"

Altman, at times, steps out of the play to remark on its emotional themes, illuminating the unconscious feelings in the room between Ronald and himself. I have to wonder if Altman would have found these comments necessary if he had been engaged in a more traditional symbolic play-based therapy. If he and Ronald had been playing with action figures or puppets, would he have felt the same need for occasional commentary? Perhaps he would have and the therapy would not have changed. But, I wonder if some of his comments come from a lingering uncertainty and discomfort that framed Altman's question at the beginning of his paper. In reading his engaging paper, I wonder what most helped Ronald. Was it Altman's reflections on the play, unique to a therapeutic space, or was it the vitality of their interactions, with all the affect of competitive sports, played out within a safe therapeutic environment?

Altman's question about sports is understandable. When thinking of seminal moments in the child therapy literature, ball playing rarely comes to mind. Images are scarce of the likes of D. W. Winnicott scoring a goal, Virginia Axline hitting a home run, or Anna Freud and Melanie Klein having a slam-dunk contest. There are however many children whose very essence may be contained in such moments on the field, and perhaps, it is our very goal in therapy to allow such children to embody these feelings in a safe but vital therapeutic space. The literature may be scant, and my own survey could be biased, but I suspect most child therapists have played ball at some point in therapy. It is, in fact, stunning that so little has been written about this work. Perhaps we need to look elsewhere for thoughts about integrating active play in child therapy. While not focused on sports, the world of dance and movement therapy may provide some inspiration. Trudi Schoop, the pioneering Dance Therapist, talked of movement and dance as a way for a person to become aware of the different parts of themselves that they embodied, encouraging people to explore the different sides of their personalities through different movements. As a comedic mime, raised in a time of Charlie Chaplin and silent films, the notion of the body as an expressive medium came naturally to Schoop, who believed that her work was the province of taking unconscious and emotional experiences and shaping them into physical form where they could find expression and integration (Schoop, 1974). Her pioneering work echoes loudly in the theories of Christine Caldwell (2003), who likewise talks about the importance of physical play and sensation to help a person embody his or her feelings and to connect those feelings to bodily experiences that promote healing. If dance and movement offer emotional expression, I wondered, how about sports? What do we express when we're playing a game of soccer or basketball?

Back in my office, as we prepared for our Real Madrid versus Tottenham match, Alex looked at me quizzically, his eyes seemingly wondering how seriously we were going to take these games. I added the color commentary, as Alex, or should I say Ronaldo, took the ball and made a couple of small feints to the left and right. I certainly wasn't going to get beaten that easily. So I stymied Alex's attempts to get by me, alerting him that we were going to have a proper go at it. In the process, I was letting Alex know that I also thought he could handle a more competitive and intense game. Alex responded in kind, his cutbacks sharper, his shielding of the ball tougher, and his tackles and forward runs increasingly physical. I played Alex competitively, though I admit to holding back a little bit. While I think the intensity of the game was crucial to allow Alex to bring forth and experience his more aggressive and competitive feelings, I think it important to add that he was eight years old and while Alex was destined to be a far more successful athlete than I, he was at a bit of a physical disadvantage at this particular time in his life. The game was intense though, as we battled back and forth, my Scottish announcer offering play-by-play to highlight the match. We finished the first half with Alex ahead by several goals, as he pushed his way through my defense and often dispossessed me when I was on the attack. "Ronaldo with another goal, just pure power on that one!" "Tottenham have it, but, no, here comes Sergio Ramos, another fine steal as he sends it along to Benzema and yet another Madrid attack, they're just coming in waves now!" My interest in this half was to both allow Alex to embody his more competitive and aggressive feelings and to invite them in and in fact, compliment them in the context of the game. There was nothing wrong with Alex's fundamental aggression. My concern was that he was not able to find a forum for his feelings, which like a pressure cooker, simmered and stewed inside.

"A classic here tonight in Madrid for this first game of this Champions League pairing. Real Madrid, as expected, playing their brand of ferocious attacking soccer. Cristiano Ronaldo running at Tottenham's defense. Can the visitors get back in this one? They've had moments of fine play but in the end, their defense has seemed a bit, well, soft in the face of Madrid's power. Perhaps they are a bit anxious playing in this new venue against such a strong and famous team."

Alex remained quiet but nodded as he passed me the ball for the second half. "And back we go as Spurs kick off! Gareth Bale with the ball now," I exclaimed as I took the ball down the right side of my carpet, side stepped my playhouse and spun inside to elude Alex's right foot, which he extended to steal the ball. "Oh, what a move by Bale!" I exclaimed, as I switched the ball to my left with an off-balance Alex in pursuit. He began to catch up to me but anticipating his move, I cut the ball back to my right, surprising both of us with that little bit of technique. "Oh, a tricky one there, what skill! He just spun him around, and that's a goal!" I proclaimed, with honest exuberance, as I slotted the ball into an empty right hand side of the goal, just clearing the bamboo basket serving as a right post. I raised my hands and headed to a corner of the office, pretending to bask in the cheers of the imagined visiting Tottenham fans who had made the trek to watch me at the Bernabéu, Madrid's stadium. Alex looked at me with disbelief, his mouth slightly ajar, his eyes sharpened. "Let's go," he declared sharply, his voice low and direct, jaw tightened and eyes steeled. In the next few seconds, he took the ball left, right, and then just directly at me, pushing me off as he headed to goal. "A very physical Madrid looks to strike back," my slightly startled announcer commented. "I say, they look a bit angered at that last goal, looking to put Spurs right back in their place!" As Alex backed into me, I slid my left foot to deflect the ball and interrupted his progress, the ball heading out of bounds under my couch.

"My ball," Alex added, as he took the ball from under the couch and set up on the right side. "Free kick, you ready? Not stopping me this time," as he bent his knees in anticipation of his next move. Until this point, Alex rarely spoke while we played soccer. Usually he just shrugged or offered a monosyllabic "Yes," "Not really," or "I don't know," to most of the things I said in our first sessions. His words now were still to the point, but at least they were getting more varied and most of all spontaneous, indicating his increasing engagement in our play together. More importantly, Alex demonstrated his feelings through our play, becoming more intensely focused in this increasingly charged second half of action. He was also tolerating a more intense game including its necessary frustration, while I used my commentator, staying in character, to note feelings that could arise. "It's my ball. Are you ready?" he half asked and half grumbled. I nodded, and the action resumed.

Real Madrid went on to defeat Tottenham Hotspur that day. Tottenham came close and made a game of it but Madrid eventually pulled away and cruised to victory. I was pleased with how the session had progressed as, via my Tottenham proxy, I had been able to engage Alex in our sessions with a new vitality. This engagement was measured nonverbally, mostly via his body language and glances. His enthusiasm far more tangible than words as we played on our makeshift soccer pitch. As time wore down, I told Alex we would need to stop in a moment, and he let out a "really?" as I explained we could play again at our next session. Alex smiled and walked out of the office with me to greet his mom. "Everything ok in there," she smiled and asked, as Alex and I looked the part of two players having just scrimmaged for over a half hour. It helped that Alex's mom had become a fan as well.

A week later, Alex came back for his next session, sat down and we chatted about his week for a few minutes, while his eyes darted in the direction of my Lego/sports equipment storage basket. As he looked, I could see his legs beginning to quiver a bit as he bounced slightly on the couch. "You look like you want to do something?" as I motioned with my hand. Without missing a beat, Alex rushed his question – "can we play soccer?" "Of course," and Alex headed to the basket, retrieved the ball, set up the goals on his side and was ready to go. "Are you going to be Tottenham again?" Alex asked. "Yup, and you?" I replied. "Real Madrid," Alex said seriously and he dropped the ball down in front of him to begin. Alex played as if we had just finished up our first game a few minutes ago and were now resuming play. I'm not sure why I was surprised. After all, kids engaged in fantasy play will regularly pick up a theme or scene from session to session. Why should sports be any different?

"Can you do the Scottish guy?" Alex asked me, with his own Scottish inflection, as he put two quick goals behind me and announced the goals himself. I was happy to do so and in a moment's notice went back to my broadcasting. To my surprise, Alex was now joining me in both playing and offering his play-by-play. I was delighted by this change. He was tentative but brave in offering his words and trying out his own version of a Scottish play-by-play commentator. Alex's energy proved infectious, and my intensity returned. Our game grew stronger and more competitive. Now, we were both playing in a Champions league knockout round. As I felt the rush of our play, perhaps fueled by my own unfulfilled sports dreams, I paused as I made a move to the right, wondering how far to take this game, memories of my own childhood basketball and baseball games coming to the fore.

Bonovitz (2009) talks about what the therapist brings to the table, as discussed in his countertransference work with Angus, a young soccer fan. In the midst of a series of soccer games, in which Bonovitz would eventually give up an early lead to a very vigilant and defensively oriented Angus, Bonovitz began to recall his own childhood sports games with a close and very competitive friend. Bonovitz recalled his own worries if the competition with his friend grew too intense, nervous that perhaps their friendship would falter. Bringing his reflections into the sessions with Angus, Bonovitz noticed how he would have a lead and then "slow down" as Angus gained momentum and the edge in their games. In a poignant moment, an honest and insightful Angus tells Bonovitz, "You're scared like other people are. I see it in your face and the way you play; you stop playing hard." In the process, Bonovitz both helped Angus notice his struggle, which he could now share with his therapist, while Bonovitz wondered about how his own fear of winning might have reinforced a more fragile self-image than he may have wanted to convey to Angus.

Bonovitz's reflections are refreshing and vivid. Every therapist was once a child, and every child has spent time, happily or not, on a gym floor, field, or pitch. Everyone has had the experience of either channeling or avoiding the aggression and competition inherent in sports. Many a child has experiences of success, failure, joy, and despair in a game. To be involved in sports means regularly dealing with feelings of pride, rage, shame, excitement, and embarrassment. For every last minute goal or winning shot, there is an awful error or mistake that rings throughout development. It is these experiences that make childhood sports memories so prominent in many of our lives. It is also why sports can offer such an impact and a ripe venue for emotional exploration in the therapeutic space.

Back in my own office, as I dribbled near my goal, I struggled with how competitive to get with Alex. What did I want from these games? Alex and I had become more competitive, dramatic, and charged in our back and forth. We also flecked the intensity of each game with humorous asides, accents, and half-time breaks.

The spring was drawing to a close, and Alex and I had developed a rhythm to our sessions. We'd chat for a little while about school and life in general, play some soccer, enjoy a half-time break where we'd chat some more or talk about soccer games from the past weekend and then continue our games. My announcer character was there for fun, but the affect existed in the room through our games. Through it all, I noticed how Alex was becoming more communicative, and lighter with respect to his feelings. We took the summer break as Alex left the city and, based on his mother's report, enjoyed a very enjoyable summer both with family and peers.

Early in September, I was scheduled for my first fall session with Alex. As I thought about seeing him again, I wondered how real life soccer drama would impact our sessions. The summer had been one of growth for Alex. I continued to follow soccer news with particular interest in the always-entertaining summer transfer season. Soccer teams can only bring in new players at two points during the year and summer is the main period in which players move, or "*transfer*," from one to another. It is a time when star players from relatively smaller teams are acquired by teams that are a step up the soccer food chain. Rumors also regularly abound involving approximately half the professional players in Europe and South America, as newspapers need to be sold and sports websites need their traffic. This is all relevant as the main drama of that particular summer transfer season centered around none other than Tottenham Hotspur, Real Madrid, and

Tottenham's superstar Gareth Bale, my main soccer persona in our sessions. After a very intense back and forth negotiation, as Tottenham desperately tried to hold onto their talisman, Bale had insisted on leaving to fulfill his own childhood fantasies, even offering a published photo of himself as an eight-year-old boy wearing a Real Madrid shirt, as evidence to disbelieving fans of his long-standing dream. To the dismay of Tottenham fans, Gareth Bale was now a member of Real Madrid, greeted warmly by thousands as he landed in Madrid and was escorted to the Bernabéu to be given his jersey and showcase a few skills. He had become Cristiano Ronaldo's sidekick. As a Spurs fan, this was an absolute disaster. I wondered what Alex would say when I saw him in the fall. I wondered what I was going to say as well.

I found out soon enough as I buzzed Alex in after the fall Labor Day weekend. Alex smiled in the waiting area, gave me a warm hello, unbuttoned a light jacket and stepped forward toward my office. As he walked, he also managed, while eyeing me, to partially spin around and show a peek at the latest Real Madrid shirt. Alex almost always wore Ronaldo's or Alonso's jersey. He also had one of the popular goalie, Iker Casillas. Not today. As Alex turned, I noticed a familiar number eleven on the back of his shirt. Gareth Bale. Yes, I was being mocked in our first session back. Game on then.

"It's good to see you again," I said. "How was your summer?" "Good to see you too, it was good, thank you for asking," Alex added with a studied politeness at the end. Alex looked at me knowingly for a second before adding, "I got a new Madrid shirt." I looked back at him, "Oh really, huh, I didn't notice," as I shifted my eyes with a slightly comedic twist. Alex followed along scrunching his eyes suspiciously, "Really, you didn't see it at all? Didn't notice anything different about my shirt?" I feigned surprise, "Nope, no, no. It looks like your shirt, you know, one of the ones you have. Very classic jersey, by the way. Looks good! Sharp!" I kept nodding as if I knew nothing. Alex raised his eyebrow, "So you didn't notice anything. Uh hmm (he looked at me dubiously) Well, it's a new one." "Really (I raised my voice enthusiastically), great, great for you. It's always great to have a new jersey, really wonderful," I smiled. Alex looked straight back at me, "Want to see the back?" "Mmmaaayy-bbbeeee," as I slowly let out the word for emphasis. "Ok, I'll turn around so you can see it. You might recognize the name," Alex nodded knowingly once more. He turned around happily to show me his new uniform featuring the name "Bale" on the back. Alex turned back around and smiled, "Do you like it?" I grumbled for a moment, squeezing my forehead for greater effect, as Alex's eyes smiled and he continued talking. "You seem a little upset today. Is it something about my jersey?" Alex asked with faux innocence, "you said you really liked it." I went into full pretend self-righteous indignation mode now, "Fine. So you got Gareth Bale. Happy now? Of all the players in the world you needed to go buy Bale huh? There was no one else available? No one? Someone who wasn't the only star left at Tottenham!?" Alex looked back at me with a smile. It was good to see him this way, in good humor and enjoying our improvisational banter. Banter can be a big part of sports, offering a good-humored bond between players. In fact, banter can be seen as its own form of play, with words serving the same function as Lego pieces, action figures, or for that matter a soccer ball. Alex's playfulness told me that he was further developing his ability to hold onto and express rather than avoid his feelings, particularly his more competitive ones. "Well, you know, Bale just belongs at Real Madrid I'm afraid. We did give you a lot of money for him and you can get some other players. Anyway, that's just how it is. It's where the best players go after all. That's life," as he shrugged his shoulders understandably toward me. "Ready to play by the way?" With that invitation, Alex made his way to our pitch and we resumed the soccer season.

I lost badly to Alex, or Gareth Bale, or whomever I played that day. He played with power and pace, reminiscent of Bale's own play. I played a dejected and dispirited Tottenham, bereft of their star player and searching for answers. I had a host of new players and in what turned out to mirror reality, Bale's replacements turned out to be very poor approximations of the genuine superstar. Alex continued to progress outside of the office as well. He continued to feel calmer at home and at school and better able to handle emotionally charged situations. Alex's mother also developed a certain skill in engaging him in a conversation where emotion could also give way to a degree of lightness. In our parenting sessions, I emphasized the idea of curiosity when dealing with Alex and his reactions. The idea of being able to wonder, without trepidation, as to why he may have felt or reacted in a certain way. It was important for Alex to experience an emotion without it always being a feeling of life or death. It was why I so much enjoyed our interplay around the Bale jersey as Alex was able to both take a step forward and backward.

Posturing and humorous boasting are staples of sports, imbuing the game with a certain energy. A certain joy. I wanted to invite Alex into this humor to help him expand his emotional range while also getting some necessary distance. In the middle of one game, I was dribbling around a bit, aimlessly, as Alex let out a fake yawn, expressing how unimpressed he was with my display. I looked up at him, "I think I'm going to join the Brazilian national team! Good idea?" Alex laughed, "You're going to do what?" "Join the Brazilians," I said nonchalantly. Alex lowered his eyes, "Brazil?" "None other," I answered affirmatively. Alex let out a sigh. "First of all, you're not actually Brazilian." I looked back at him and replied earnestly, "But in my heart, I feel I am." Alex rolled his eyes, "In your heart?" He sighed again, "I thought you felt you were Scottish?" "Well, I have many feelings you know, don't we all?" Alex now put his hand on his head feigning disbelief, "Ok, whatever. But your name is Henry Kronensomething. That's not a Brazilian name." I popped right back, "Not to worry, I've got that all sorted out." Alex looked up at the ceiling, "Yes? What is it?" I looked back at him for a second, a big smile on my face as I continued dribbling, "Henrinho!" "Henrinho," Alex said with disbelief, chuckling beside himself. "It's good, right?" I continued as I lost control of the ball. "Right, listen Henrinho, I think the players on Brazil can dribble a ball without losing it under the sofa." I gestured recognition as to the point, "True, but I lost the ball with style. That's just as important as actually controlling it," I continued blithely. "No, actually it's not as important," Alex suggested before continuing, "Never mind. Are you ever going to make a move with the ball? By the way, I'm getting sleepy." I looked in mock horror, "Sleepy! Sleepy! No one sleeps playing with Henrinho!" I made a sharp move, as Alex calmly poked the ball away and took possession. He looked back at me, "Uh-huh, sure. Henrinho." Alex wasn't used to humor in his life. Of course he enjoyed slapstick and funny shows, but the idea of humor as a way to lighten moments of intensity, to take something off of painful moments of awareness, was new to him, and he took comfort in our banter. The humor allowed him to play with his own skills and challenges without feeling so threatened. I admit there was a dual purpose to our games and our back and forth. On one hand, I wanted to use soccer as a dramatic forum to help Alex immerse himself further in feelings that he avoided. On the other hand, I wanted to use our burgeoning humor and broadcasting as a way to get some distance from those feelings. The two approaches could easily weave in and out during the course of a session or fixture. We could jump into or out of the competitive fray as seemed fit.

Also, our games were becoming more expansive in addition to competitive. My choice of the Brazilians was more than coincidental, as they are known for their sense of soccer as an art form as much as a competition. Alex and I didn't just try to score goals now but to score impressive ones. We aspired to a stylishness, with tricks, moves, and fancy dribbling. We used the desk, couch, and goalposts as not just sidelines and boundaries, but for passes and deflections that spoke to our burgeoning creativity. My area rug was now serving both as floor for comfortable play and as a canvas for expressiveness and soccer artistry. Ok, we weren't that good, but the point is that there was a new expressive medium in our play, allowing us to try out moves and extend ourselves in a manner which we hadn't previously.

I still wondered how far I wanted to take the competitive element though. Alex had won every game as I would play him up to a certain point but then back off a little bit. I sensed that I could take the competition too far for Alex and overwhelm him. But, was that really the case or was I scared to go deeper into exploring Alex's darker feelings? We all have our style of play, and mine, while competitive, has always relied on a measure of humor and absurdism as a counterweight to the seriousness of a game. I wondered, was I allowing my own style to get in the way at this point? Was my humor making the affect tolerable for Alex, or was it diluting the intensity of the feelings and our interactions that we needed to explore?

I decided that it was time to take the drama a step further. Winning and losing games in therapy has been the subject of much discussion in the child therapy literature (Barish, 2010). In general, discussions emphasize how winning is crucial for many kids' self-esteem so the therapist should respect that need. However, the therapist doesn't want to convey a sense of the child as too fragile, or collude excessively with a child's avoidance of difficult feelings that may come with losing. In other words, it's a therapist's discretion as to what he or she thinks a child may need at a given moment. More importantly, the therapeutic work is to find a way to focus less on the actual winning and losing and more on the feelings, which a child must navigate in his or her daily life. In my mind, Alex and I had been playing for some months, and I felt his ability to engage and handle intense feelings was continuing to grow. With his increasing use of humor and expansiveness in our games, I felt Alex was communicating a sense of joy in our play. There was a creativity and a calm for Alex. I also started to feel that I was holding back again, and as Alex grew, I wanted to work with him more honestly. I wasn't sure who was going to win our next game, but I decided that, as long as I sensed Alex could handle the situation, I would play harder in our next session and see how things progressed.

But how hard would I actually play? I may not be much of a player, but my size advantage meant that I could probably defeat Alex if I wanted to. Was that my new goal? To use the spirit of therapeutic authenticity to defeat an eight-year-old boy who had come to my office? I would hope not. But, then how authentic was I actually going to be, and how could I meet Alex or another child for that matter in a place that brought an emotional charge, while being honest about the fact that I was holding back? I don't presume to have a clear answer for my conundrum, other than an openness to its complexity.

Alex and I began our next session with some fancy moves and an entertaining game was deadlocked 2–2 early in the first half. I played more competitively with Alex and he matched my intensity. The result was a lower score than usual as we each played stronger, particularly on defense. We each added a couple more goals and went into the half-time break at 4–4, as we sat down for a quick break. "Not a bad half, there, eh?" I wondered aloud to Alex. "Yeah, pretty good. I'll pull ahead though," Alex returned. "Maybe, but you have to get through my airtight defense," I boasted with the accent on airtight for emphasis. Alex looked at me with a smirk, "Airtight," as he mimicked my enunciation, "we'll see how airtight your defense is in the second half. I already megged you three times already," Alex continued, referring to a '*nutmeg*' where one player dribbles the ball between the defender's legs while maintaining possession. For a player on offense, a nutmeg reflects great skill while the defender is left feeling duped. Alex and I drank some water, chatted a couple more minutes and got back on the pitch, also known as my area rug, for the second-half action.

Alex quickly grabbed the lead, as he flicked the ball off a sofa edge and angled it past for a goal. Alex raised his hands in triumph, celebrating his goal. Not to be outdone, I passed the ball off my desk past Alex, and managed to collect it as I sped down the left side and scored into the open goal to tie the game. I too raised my hands in triumph, pausing for a moment to applaud my pinpoint passing and cleverness. The intensity was building. Alex gave me a slightly impressed and annoyed look and took control. We went back and forth, each of us scoring, and playing tough defense as the game seesawed. Alex went up by one, I'd tie it up. He'd look like he was going to break ahead, but I'd pull even again. We stayed focused. With a few minutes left, we were tied up at fifteen. Alex had the ball, his face slightly red from running around, his eyes locked on the ball. I played just as seriously. As we played, the only sound in the room was of the two of us running around and the ball rolling off our feet across the floor, hitting a wall, basket, or sofa. The only words between us now were scoring updates. Alex spun around and shot toward my goal, the ball missing wide as I took control with time starting to run down. Alex looked nervous, his usually steady defense getting reckless as he tried to win the ball back. I glided past his challenge and saw an opening to score. I had taken leads before but never this late in the game and never at such an intense moment. Alex looked like he was getting overwhelmed, as I quickly decided whether to go for goal or hold back. Writing about it now makes the action seem slower and more intentional than it was at that moment. In the game, I had about a second to decide whether to shoot or not.

I took the lead 16–15, as I rolled the ball into an open corner of the makeshift goal. "How much time left?" Alex plaintively asked, his voice getting pressured. "A couple of minutes," I replied. He quickly took the ball out and started to move with it. He was too quick now. Too forceful. Too pressured. I could see he was going to lose his head and force shots. I had wanted to heighten the drama in our sessions but I didn't want to overwhelm Alex. I decided to bring back my announcer to help him through the moment, as a third character could help him take a step back from the intensity. I did the Scottish accent but without the cartoonish elements that felt ill-suited to this moment. "Madrid with the ball. They certainly sense the urgency now. Down by one. They do have time though and will look to keep their composure and play their game. Not an easy task though as the fans are on their feet waiting to see this finale! Possible history in the making here at the Bernabéu tonight!" With that, Alex steadied himself just enough. He bowled past me, using his physicality for a tough-earned but certainly legitimate goal: 16–16.

How far to take this? How much drama is good and how much is too much? I took the ball and controlled. This time Alex was more careful, avoiding any unnecessary lunges that would let me run by him. He knew I liked to make quick moves and cuts to create distraction, and he wasn't going to go for my fakes or passes off the desk so easily. But he played it a little too safe. I went left, and Alex, expecting me to cut back right, gave me the space. I took advantage, sped past him and angled the ball into the goal: 17–16. Just moments remaining.

I decided to stick with the announcing as a way to help narrate some of the feelings in the room. At a moment when we were at odds on the pitch, my announcer kept me connected to Alex and his feelings. "Just incredible. Breathtaking back and forth action here tonight. A match truly for the ages. Tottenham calm on the attack. Now Madrid ready to answer. Fans in the crowd standing, mouths open, wondering what will happen next. What more can happen in this match?! We've seen everything so far!" Alex pushed ahead again. "Cristiano with the ball. He looks to push forward, but Spurs' defense tightens. Michael Dawson holds him. Not the greatest talent but always tough on defense. A true English defender if ever there was one. Have to wonder if Madrid may need to use some of their skill as well." With that, Alex, did a stepover, a trick to fake me, a couple of cuts, and took advantage of my misstep, as he slotted the ball behind me. He didn't have time to celebrate, immediately going into a pressing position on defense: 17–17.

I took the ball and seeing the pressure coming, managed to pass off the far corner of my desk. We both scrambled for the ball, which fell kindly at my feet, as a surprise bounce sent it skipping past Alex. With a moment's hesitation, I took it on my left foot, changed direction slightly to my right, as Alex went the other way: 18–17. Tottenham up by one.

Alex immediately took the ball and shot before my announcer could speak. I knew how much time we had left. I had a plan to mix up the emotional drama and emotional distance. I didn't actually have a plan about the outcome though. In truth, I hadn't expected to pull off the moves I had made, but here I was. Up by a goal with barely any time left. I wanted to stay connected to Alex, but he reacted too quickly after my goal. He spun and looked to shoot. With the pressure in him rising, Alex didn't set his feet correctly and his powerful shot was too hurried. At that moment, the emotion of the game had taken over completely. His powerful shot missed wide.

Alex was shocked. His eyes grew wider, and his reddened face contorted, as I retrieved the ball. "No!! No!! How much time! How much time?" He cried. I looked directly at him to make eye contact in that moment. I didn't use my announcer because I felt I needed to directly reach Alex. "About a minute," I said clearly, as I shook my head to try to calm him. "Settle on defense now, it's my ball. You can take a breath if you need to." "There's no time," Alex exclaimed as his eyes welled. "There's time," I said, trying to calm him, "Not much but enough. Do what you need." Alex steadied himself. "Ready?" I asked as Alex nodded up and down.

It was at this point that I realized fully that unless I went out of my way to lose, Alex and I were going to make a piece of our own history that day. We were almost out of time. I would have possession and then Alex would have maybe one quick chance with the ball. I wasn't sure if I had pushed the competition too far. I also didn't want to go out of my way to purposely lose the game as I was concerned about what I was going to communicate to Alex if just let him win at this point. I wanted to convey that however difficult, I believed he could handle the emotion and intensity of our game. I was worried that letting Alex win at this point would send a message that

I thought he was too fragile. But I certainly wasn't sure. I looked over at the clock and the session was at an end. Alex and I often had a countdown at the end of a game and I said we had ten seconds left. Alex stiffened. I took possession, and with my ambivalence on display, lost the ball with three seconds remaining on the clock.

Alex took the ball again. "Three." He spun and tried a quick move. "Two." He took a shot that bounced off my leg but directly back to Alex. "One." He looked to control the ball, mishandling it as it rolled to the sofa. "Zero." We looked at each other for a second. We were in uncharted territory. Then Alex kept going, took the ball and went toward my goal and put it through after time had elapsed. He cried out, "That counted, that counted! I scored! It was a tie! A tie!" I looked at Alex again. I thought about what to say or do. Alex was so upset. I steadied myself and said a bit too calmly, "I think it was after the clock ran out." "No! Uh-uh! No!" Alex's face was getting redder. At that moment, he wasn't playing a game. "It was a goal. It counted! Tie game!" I decided to engage in the back and forth about his disputed goal for a few seconds. "Whoa, whoa, whoa. I said zero," I suggested. "No, it was a mistake," Alex countered. "There was still time. No!"

It was certainly one way for Alex to handle the outcome of our game and true to real sports, with a disputed ending to conclude the drama. With more time I could have settled Alex, perhaps as we analyzed an imaginary replay of the goal and timer, to give us a couple of moments to digest the intensity of the ending. I wanted us to have a little more time but our session had gone over, I had another child waiting, and I thought I needed to trust my relationship with Alex. As with our game, these decisions have to be made quickly, however composed they may seem in the retelling. We ended our session as an unhappy looking Alex left my office and headed to his mother in the waiting area.

I had several more sessions that afternoon and evening and admit to my distraction. I kept thinking back to Alex. Did I really need to win a silly soccer game? Even if winning was the right way to go, couldn't I have given us a little time at the end to deal with the fallout instead of ending the game when our time was up? I was annoyed with myself. I also didn't have time in between appointments that day, so I planned to give Alex's mom a heads-up at the end of the day, just to let her know about the ending of our session in case anything came up at home. I needn't have worried. After finishing my last appointment I listened to my answering machine messages. Alex's mom had called wondering if anything had happened in our session because Alex was in an awful mood and had been screaming and berating her the entire way home from the office. I called her back and explained what had happened. Alex's mom was very understanding but worried if he would come back next week. I told her I had the same fear but that's all it was. A fear. Alex and I had worked together for a year and I trusted in our relationship. Fear and its anxious and angry offshoots had been a crucial part of our work together. The work of therapy was to help Alex see that he would be ok even if a feeling was strong and overwhelming. The feeling would pass and he would be stronger for it.

This conversation was based on the idea that Alex would actually arrive at his session and talk to me. While I trusted he would, I couldn't be certain. After all, difficult moments can also be experienced as ruptures, and a promising therapy can hit a standstill. Then again, avoiding any dissonance in a therapy is itself a standstill, and part of therapy is helping a child as he or she experiences complicated feelings. The question was whether I had misread or lost my connection to Alex in that last session. To think he wouldn't have a reaction was foolish. But what about my timing? Should I have pushed the competition but at the end kept it a tie at least, sensing Alex's upset? Would that have been more gradual and digestible for Alex? I would have to wait until next week to find out.

I also had to manage my own anxiety. I felt like checking in with Alex's mom but also felt it wasn't fair to do so. Whatever happened in that session and in the sessions leading up to it was between Alex and me. The outcome of our last session should be between us as well. I also hadn't heard from his mom in the ensuing days so I was going to trust our relationship and expect to see Alex at our next session. I was still worried though.

I expected to see Alex at 3pm the following Tuesday. I walked out and saw him waiting with his mom. I said hello to a quiet Alex and gestured for him to come in. He followed, walked in and sat on the couch as usual. I welcomed him back and he nodded. "Last appointment was pretty intense," I said. Alex looked up for a second uncomfortably, his facial expression blank, his body clenched. I continued, "You looked um, how should I put, it, upset, unhappy, ummh, maybe even angry?" "It's ok," Alex muttered quickly. I paused for a second, enough to feel I could speak calmly but directly, engaging Alex rather than sounding too clinical and disembodied. "It doesn't have to be," I continued. "To be what?" Alex wondered. "Ok." I paused again. "It doesn't have to be ok." I paused again and looked at Alex who relaxed slightly and looked back at me. I chose to interpret his look and body language as an invitation to continue talking. "What I mean is it's ok if you're angry at me. Or maybe angry at yourself because I won the last game. It's a feeling. We all get that way sometimes and it's kind of, well, you know, healthy. We can talk about it a bit, don't worry, not too much, I know that's not totally your thing, but the idea is that we can a have a lot of feelings in here. We can also enjoy ourselves and get into our games, and if you're upset sometimes, well, (as I gestured with my hands), so, you're upset. We'll figure it out." I looked at Alex again, who was lounging on the couch at this point, looking more relaxed, the tension slipping out of his body. He paused for a second himself now. I wondered what he would say about my monologue. I wondered how much he would talk about his feelings from the last session.

"Are you done?" he said very calmly and nonchalantly. A bit taken aback I muttered, "Well, yeah sort of." "That's a relief," answered Alex, who was rolling his eyes. I looked back and decided to play along, "What do you mean 'that's a relief'?" as I rolled my own eyes for emphasis. "Nothing," Alex said. I looked back at him with eyes wide, "Uh-huh, all right out with it. That was a very meaningful thing I said." Alex let out a soft smile, "You mean your (and now Alex put his hands up to make quotation marks) speech. Uh-huh, very powerful. Yup. I'll always remember it." I feigned shock, "You're mocking me!" Alex smiled, "No, no. Not at all. It was really great. You know, your, (he did the quotation marks again) speech."

So we were back to banter. Sensing a stronger Alex, I decided to take our back and forth a bit further. "You're just upset." Alex looked back, "Oh really. What do I have to be upset about." I puffed out my chest and blustered, "Because of my, (pausing for effect, my eyes looking upward to some imaginary horizon in my office) victory!" Alex chortled, "Please. I've beaten you a million times. Anyway it was a tie." "A tie? I don't think so my Real Madrid friend. That's was a bona fide, fantastic, amazing upset win for, moi." I was clearly playing this up now and was delighted with our own unique processing of the last session. I was also wary that I'd need to wind it down at some point too. "Moi," Alex sweetly mocked me, "Wow. Just wow. Anyway, I tied it at the end." "Did not!" I argued. "Yup," as Alex ignored my protest, "I scored at the end." "After time ran out!" I said. "Nope," Alex insisted. "Yup." "Nope." "Yup." "Nope." This was starting to get ridiculous. Alex and I just looked at each other and started to set up the goals again. We had talked plenty of the last session. We did it by staying in character as soccer players, as was true of our work together on the makeshift soccer pitch. Our sessions did shift following my victory. It wasn't so much about whether I won any other games, which did happen a couple of times. We never did agree on the final outcome of that game with Alex insisting he had tied it in regulation time before the end of the session. I didn't really care at that point. What mattered was that Alex was discovering that he didn't need to be as afraid of his feelings. Of messing up or getting too upset. These challenges didn't disappear but they kept improving. There were later sessions when Alex talked more directly about his feelings, including a poignant one where he questioned whether he actually was a good player and if I just let him make his moves. I would later learn this occurred after some difficulty he experienced in a real-life game with some friends.

For Alex and me, soccer became our venue much the way a castle, canvas, or a sandbox becomes for other children. It is not for nothing that aesthetically pleasing soccer players and teams are known as expressive. The same goes for any sport, be it baseball, basketball, hockey. Whatever the child's natural medium will allow for expression, and in a therapeutic space, a natural environment in which a child can play out his or her internal worlds. Not just as a blank canvas though, but rather, in the context of a relationship that both allows for, facilitates, and helps a child express and integrate so many different feelings, particularly for a child such as Alex, who expresses so much through his body and through physical activity. In that respect, Alex is just a representative for a host of children whose psychological and emotional experiences may be rooted in the physical. It may be hard for us, as verbal and often heady adults, to always appreciate the role of the physical and nonverbal in our work. We take for granted the use of words and conscious symbols to mediate our experience. However, we also may realize how different we may feel when we are able to integrate our bodies into our daily experience. Those are moments when earlier experiences, perhaps from long ago, are rekindled. We don't need to play ball with every child who walks into a child therapy office. Many children have little interest in such games. But others do. Some children are naturally athletic just as others are artistic, their bodies moving through space as a poet's words on a page. I think it is important that we respect the place of a child's interest and experience and find a way to enter into that child's world while trusting that in doing so, we will have the opportunity for a therapeutic journey that offers emotional richness and lessons for both therapist and child, regardless of the therapeutic venue. It is remarkable what can happen from playing around with a squishy little soccer ball.

6   The Princess and Dal Bhat Tarkari

ME: Princess, Princess, I'm here to rescue you (I say as I barge into the castle dungeon).

ALMA: Hi prince. Quick we have to get out of here, the witch is nearby and her guards are everywhere. I know a good spot we can hide. C'mon let's go (as she points toward the side of the castle).

ME: Ok, are you alright? I missed you.

ALMA: Yeah, I'm fine. But hurry, we've got to get away from here.

ME: Right, let's go. Umm, where are we going?

ALMA: To the inn. It's in the middle of the forest. We can hide there for the night and then head back home tomorrow.

ME: (I pause to consider the idea. I also have a feeling that I know where this is heading as I nod my assent to Alma's plan.) To the inn! Let's go. (We hurry to the inn, have a seat and make plans to get some food.) I'll go to the innkeeper and bring back some food for us to eat. What would you like?

ALMA: Anything. I'm starving.

ME: Ok, I'll be back in a minute. (I walk over to talk to the pretend innkeepers, get some pretend bread, chicken, and water, and head back to the princess.)

ALMA: (gestures to me to come over to the side of the room as she wants to tell me something. She leans and says in a whisper) Henry, you came back but the princess is gone.

ME: (whispering) Gone? Where did she go?

ALMA: She's gone. Just gone. You have to figure that out. She disappears. The witch's guards must have found her or the witch cast a spell and brought her back to the castle.

ME: Seriously?

ALMA: Seriously. She's gone again.

As Alma played out her assertive princess my mind wandered back a decade, to a similar scene played out with Sarah.

SARAH: Henry, you're the brother. Now look, you see this house over here. There are five different rooms. Each one is used for something special in the house. The sister's bedroom is here and you go looking around for her but she's not there. You have to try to find her but she's not around. Ok?

ME: Ok. What do I do once I can't find her?

SARAH: You get very worried and start calling the police.

ME: Do they find her?

SARAH: No. And anyway, you have to play the game. Ok, now let's start, you start looking for me.

ME: Ok, I'm looking. (My eyes search around the room.) Hmm, I wonder where she could be? Hello! Where are you? Are you in the house? (I search the area.) She's not there. Where could she be? Where has she gone? I hope she's ok.

SARAH: Now you call the police.

ME: (I pick up an imaginary telephone.) Hello police. I need some help. I can't find my sister. I've looked everywhere.

SARAH: (Takes on the deep voice of an imagined police officer on the other end of the line). Hello. This is the police.

ME: Hi, can you help me. I can't find my sister. She's supposed to be home but she's gone and I can't find her (my voice becomes more plaintive). I've looked everywhere.

SARAH: You have to keep looking for her.

ME: (Surprised) Yes, but I'm calling for help. I need some help finding my sister. You see, she's disappeared.

SARAH: I can't really help. Sorry. You need to find her. But don't worry. You will.

ME: I'm glad you think so. I just don't know where she is. Well, ok then. I'll keep looking. (I hang up the phone and resume searching. As I look, Sarah motions for me to look near the closet area of the office, next to a large brown desk chair where she's hiding.) Hmm. I think I saw something moving over there. Maybe it's her? Sister, sister, is that you? It's me.

SARAH: Yeah, hi, I was wondering when you were going to find me.

ME: Well, I didn't know where to look. What were you doing here anyway?

SARAH: I had to get away. I'll explain it all later but for now, let's just get back home.

ME: Ok, let's head back. I can't wait to hear the whole story. (As we walk back, Sarah whispers to me.)

SARAH: She disappears again.

ME: Again. But she was just with me. How did she disappear?

SARAH: She just does. Then you have to go find her again.

ME: That's a lot of searching.

SARAH: Yeah, I know. You'll find her again.

Alma's and Sarah's play is rich and evocative, reflecting a child's journey as she tries to make sense of where she comes from, where she is going, and how she got there. What is also remarkable about the vignettes is that on appearance, they could involve the same child. Instead, the stories and themes were voiced by different children, who I worked with at different times, spanning a period of ten years. The similarity of the children's play speaks volumes about common themes among children as well as the role of play in helping a child better understand and explore questions and feelings about his or her past.

My discussion about the children in this chapter is not meant to be exhaustive regarding therapy with children who have been adopted across cultures and the attachment difficulties that pose a challenge to the families and therapist alike. Rather, it is meant to consider an element of working with children that frequently arises within play and how play, along with other expressive mediums, can serve as a powerful vehicle to foster a child's development and healthy transition to his or her adopted family.

When Sarah first began, she was nearly four years old, and was living with her adopted parents as well as another adopted brother. Her brother, nine years old, struggled with explosive behavior. Sarah was an unusually verbal child who regularly spoke to her mother about her brother's challenges and used to watch him like a hawk, lest he lose control without anyone noticing. Sarah's precociousness had served her well in life and she was often praised for her maturity and intelligence. Of course there was another side to staying so vigilant, as Sarah was very controlled, rarely expressed her feelings to other people, and as can be seen in the above vignette was most comfortable directing others.

Ten years later, Alma walked into my office as a most poised, verbal, and precocious four-year-old. She played, chatted, painted, danced, and smiled. In short, she did everything one could imagine to be a good play partner. She was incredibly charming, funny, and creative. I thought how much I enjoyed our session and how much fun it was to spend time with Alma, and how much she reminded me of Sarah from so many years earlier. How unusual for these children to occupy this particular place in therapy and in my own mind. Working with each of them was great fun as their sessions were creative and rich. At the same time I wondered, was their ability to connect so easily in their initial sessions part of the reason they were seeing me? Other children would begin sessions warily, careful not to stray too far from their parents. But these children were so different.

The answer seemed connected to their attachment histories and a change in each child's early experience. In a healthy situation, children born to biological parents typically become attached to those parents, depending on them for nurturance and support, while enjoying their time with each parent in a way that is both loving and reciprocal. There are of course lapses in a child's attachment to his or her parents but a typically developing and healthy child develops a secure attachment (Bowlby, 1973, 1982; Ainsworth, 1978), where a child feels safe in the presence of his or her parents and gradually internalizes that feeling of safety to explore the world. In a child's younger years, he or she is most comfortable with caregivers and is careful when meeting new people. In Alma's case, she hadn't developed this sort of connection at a younger age. She had been raised first in an orphanage and then a loving foster family in the Himalayan Mountains. Alma's unusual ability to solicit attention, to lodge herself into another person's world, and to make that person want to get to know her had likely contributed to her winding up with a new loving mother in New York City. Her ability to engage others with such impressive skill and fearlessness stood out. She had come from a different part of the world and had developed a capacity to stand out from other children. These skills proved most useful on first impression, making initial sessions and meetings memorable. Based on my own experience in my initial session with Alma, I can only imagine how her adopted mother felt during and after their first meeting. Alma's adaptive abilities were extraordinary.

But, at what cost? What happened after the shine of the first meeting wore off? This little girl worked so hard to impress and engage others, presenting more as a young adult than a small child. What happened when she needed to be a child again? Could she? Perhaps there was a reason why Alma also couldn't sleep at night, calling as a younger child might, for her mother's comfort. Perhaps there was a reason why Alma could become so distraught at times. When her mother didn't respond with perfect empathy, Alma would say that she shouldn't have been adopted and didn't deserve to have a mommy. While some of Alma's declarations may have been tinged with drama, her upset was real and spoke to a lingering insecurity that periodically broke into an inconsolable flow of tears.

The ever-vigilant, mature, and articulate Sarah kept watch over everyone and everything in her home. At school Sarah adopted the role of a teacher's assistant, with a particular eye on helping struggling classmates. Once, she personally referred a preschool classmate of hers to me who was struggling with tantrums. I had never before nor since received a referral from a four-year-old. At the same time, Sarah also complained of headaches, stomach pain, and various other bodily ailments. For a highly verbal child, she was very uncomfortable expressing her feelings and when upset, would become overwhelmed and shut down. In one memorable episode, Sarah became upset at school and fell to the floor seemingly unconscious. Her teachers, worried Sarah had a concussion or possible seizure, immediately sought medical attention as attendants tried to figure out what happened and why Sarah was unresponsive. It was only an hour later when her mother came to the doctor's office and spoke to her daughter that Sarah opened her eyes, lifted her head, stood up, grabbed her backpack, and calmly walked out the door to head home. She had been awake the entire time.

In the case of each girl, her play offered detail as to what she was struggling with, both in terms of her attachment and her confusion over early experiences. Alma's play began quickly, as did Sarah's. In our early sessions Alma directed a version of her story about a princess who had been captured by an evil witch, was saved by the prince, was recaptured by the witch, saved by the prince, and on and on. Alma played this game repetitively at home, though she maintained her enthusiasm no matter how many times she played out the drama.

ALMA: I'll be the princess and you'll be the prince. Oh, and I'll be the witch also, and you can play some of the guards, ok?

ME: Ok.

ALMA: (In a most industrious mode, sets up the castle and characters in exact positions) Ok, I'm the princess now and you're the prince and we're about to get married. Ready, ok.

ME: Ok. What I am supposed to do?

ALMA: (In a friendly but assertive voice) You're supposed to ask the princess to marry her and then you'll walk back to all the people to tell them you're getting married, and they'll start to get everything ready for the big wedding, but before they have the wedding, the witch, she's going to set up a trap for them, and she'll capture the princess, and she'll bring the princess back to her house and keep her there. Ok?

ME: Yup, I think I have that (as I'm impressed but also surprised by Alma's strength and efficiency).

ALMA: Good, let's go. Ok, c'mon.

ME: Right, oh, yes. Hello princess, it is so wonderful to see you today. My princess, my princess, would you like to marry me?

ALMA: (maintains her friendly voice) No, no, you're supposed to do that in this part of the castle, and you don't say would you like to marry me, you say, 'come princess, let's get married'.

ME: Ok, come princess let's get married.

ALMA: Right, but you do that when we start the play, not yet.

ME: I was just practicing.

ALMA: Ok, let's start.

ME: Oh, hello princess. (I look back at Alma to make sure I'm getting this right) Princess?

ALMA: Yes (she says expectantly, waving with her hand to cue me).

ME: Come, let's get married.

ALMA: Ok. (Alma now gives me directions about where we're supposed to go to prepare for the wedding). Now, we move over to this part of the castle, but the witch is going to be waiting for us.

ME: Ok, let's walk over there to get married my princess.

ALMA: (Continues directing) We walk over here (Alma points to the back of the castle) and then the witch pops out and gets the princess.

ME: Got it.

ALMA: Ok, now we're walking.

ME: Yes, we're walking. Soon, princess, we shall be married.

ALMA: (She now takes on the scary voice of the witch, who has appeared near the castle walls). Not so fast. Ha, ha. Away, prince, the princess is mine (back to her regular voice as Alma). The witch takes the princess away and disappears. Now, you're supposed to go look for her. Everyone is looking for her. But, they can't find her.

ME: Where has the princess gone? This is the work of that evil witch! Ah, I must find her. I must find my princess. I shall look over there, in the mountains (as I point to the sofa in my office).

Alma's play was notable for its theme of a missing princess, a witch who wanted the princess for herself, and a beloved prince who was looking to rescue her. Her play was also notable for Alma's great detail and precise stage and dialogue directions. At the same time that Alma gave me instructions as to what I was supposed to say, there hadn't been as much actual dialogue in our scenes. In the process, Alma hadn't given much of a clue as to the emotions behind our scenes and characters. She also hadn't given me much room to enter into her play as much as to follow her direction. Perhaps Alma was trying very hard to control these emotions, reflecting various degrees of loss and longing, or maybe she wasn't yet aware of them. In any event, the lack of emotional content may have been why Alma kept repeating this story in our early sessions and in her play at home with her mother. Maybe she was trying to locate the feelings that likely resonated in her own experience but wasn't able to. Instead, she had latched onto this familiar fairy tale as a sort of proxy of her own experiences. I saw our play as an opportunity for Alma to begin to either better understand or allow for her emotional world to register and to allow someone else to enter into her emotional world with her. Now that I was the prince doing the searching, I had a bit more space to operate in our session. I expected that while Alma would offer direction, I could begin to narrate my own experience as I looked for the princess, and in the process start to introduce more emotional themes into our play.

ME: Princess, princess. Oh, princess, my beloved princess, where are you? Where could you be? Where did that wretched witch take you? What has she done? (I search around unsuccessfully.) Ahh! (I let out a sound that tries to capture both sadness and anger.) Princess? (I look around the sofa/mountain area longer.) She's not here. This used to be the witch's lair. She must have moved and is holding my princess somewhere else. I will check back near the castle, maybe there is some sort of magic area she has come up with. Those witches. Terrible creatures!

ALMA: He's going to look for her over there. But she's not there either. But then, he goes to the forest and he hears a sound and he realizes the princess is close by so he looks over here (she points near a playhouse in my office) and then he sees the witch's house and he rescues the princess. But then, they run away and they stop at a place where they get something to eat and drink and the witch's guards are there looking for them and the guards recognize the prince and the princess and they have to run and some people at the place try to help the prince and princess but other people try to stop them.

ME: Got it.

ALMA: Ok. Csshhh! (Alma makes a noise to show me the princess is nearby)

ME: Wait a second. I'm still over here near the castle. I haven't even walked over to the forest yet. (I do this as I'm trying to slow this scene down. To allow it to simmer and resonate rather than just playing out the details so quickly.)

ALMA: Ok, well, go over there then.

ME: I'm going to head over to the forest, maybe I can find the princess over there. Oh, princess! Princess! Where are you?

ALMA: (Looks at me) Ok, now I'm going to make the sound and you'll go and realize it's the princess.

ME: (I nod my head) Yes, I remember. I've got it. Go ahead, do the 'cshhh' sound thing.

ALMA: (Smiles) Csshh! Csshh!

ME: Two sounds!

ALMA: Just go ahead.

ME: What was that! A squirrel? A rabbit? An owl flying in the forest? Or, maybe it was a sign, a message! Perhaps the princess is nearby. I'm looking for her (my voice starts to slow down and lowers to a whisper). Maybe I'll hear another clue.

ALMA: (In a faint tiny voice) Help, Help!

ME: I hear her. She's out there. Shh. I'll walk quietly and listen. (I put my hand to my ear and walk carefully through the office.)

ALMA: In here. Over here. It's me. She stuck me in the dungeon.

ME: Here I come. (I arrive at the dungeon.) Princess, it's me! I'm here to rescue you!

ALMA: (starts directing me) Now they escape and run back to the castle.

ME: (Here I decided to nudge Alma to stay in our play. To stay with the emotion of the story rather than its direction.) Wait a minute. I was in character.

ALMA: They escape.

ME: Yeah, but I was ready to act the whole thing out.

ALMA: So they try to get married again.

ME: But the escape?

ALMA: (Looks at me sympathetically) Ok. Let's go ahead.

ME: (In a pleased voice) Great. Ok, um, where were we?

ALMA: You were rescuing the princess.

ME: Right, ok, back to our places. I'm …

ALMA: You're outside the dungeon and I'm in the dungeon and you rescue me and then we run away but the witch chases after us with her guards. We get to this inn where there's a place to eat and drink and stay there but the guards find us and then …

ME: (I playfully put my hands up, urging Alma to slow down a bit) I was kind of 'in the rescue moment' you know. Like, this whole thing is a little way ahead here, can I just, well, I mean no disrespecting the story, which of course is quite fascinating, but can we get back to the rescue?

I feel like I'm kind of focused on that part right now and then we can get to the rest of the story.

ALMA: Well, ok. Go ahead. Just remember where they go next.

ME: Totally. I got it. Clear on this. After the rescue, they go to the inn, get chased, the whole thing.

ALMA: Good. Ok, go ahead.

ME: Ok. (I pause for a minute as I'm feeling we went a little far afield. I also want to make sure I haven't lost Alma in my wish to keep the scene going.)

ALMA: Well?

ME: Sorry, just taking a second to get back into the scene. I was looking for you, just found you in the dungeon after you called out and now I'm trying to rescue you. Just getting back into the feeling.

ALMA: Can we just go ahead?

ME: Yes, yes. Just a second more. I'm the prince and I just found you. Kind of a mix of excitement and... and...

ALMA: You're happy to find me but you were also scared

ME: (My eyes open wider) That's good. That works.

ALMA: (Sighs) Let's go.

ME: Ready. (My voice rises) Princess, I'm here, I'm here to rescue you. Oh, I thought I'd never find you again. (I look around) We need to figure out a way out of here.

ALMA: The lock on the door is on the side. Open the lock and I can get free. But beware of the witch.

ME: (I fumble with the lock, making a few sounds of annoyance as I work at it.) Almost got it princess. Almost. Getting there.

ALMA: Try turning it (she motions with her hand) that way.

ME: Got it. C'mon princess, let's get out of this place before the witch finds out and tries to catch us.

ALMA: Ok, so now they run to the inn and ...

ME: (I sigh) We're in character here you know.

ALMA: Oh, all right. All right.

ME: Let's go princess, through the forest. There's an inn at the edge of the forest. We can stop there to rest and eat something before we return to the castle. Princess, I can't believe I found you, I was worried the witch had made you vanish or put some sort of spell on you.

ALMA: She tried to. (Now Alma is using her hands to gesture as she talks) She tried to put this spell on me to make me fall asleep forever but I wouldn't let her because I had learned magic to keep her from being able to put me under a spell.

ME: Magic? Hmm, what form of powerful magic is this that you learned princess?

ALMA: Just magic. I learned it from the fairies in the forest when I was younger.

ME: Remarkable. Very powerful this magic is. Fairies, huh?

ALMA: (She points to one of the chairs in the office) There's the inn.

ME: Yes, there it is. It will be good to get a chance to rest. All this running around has left me tired.

ALMA: I know, me too. And I'm more tired and hungry because I was stuck in the dungeon all that time you know. Let's go inside. (Alma gives me some more information as to our setting) Ok, so there are a lot of people inside and it's noisy and we sit down to have something to eat and drink but then the witch's guards come in and they're looking for us.

ME: Ok. (back into character) I take a bit of pretend food and a drink from a pretend glass. Oh it's good to eat something. I'm sorry princess, you must be really hungry and tired, are you ok?

ALMA: Yes, I'm ok now. (Starts to look worried) But look over there, I know those two guys. They work for the witch! We've got to get out of here!

ME: Uh oh, c'mon let's go out this way (we run to the side of the castle trying to elude our pursuers).

ALMA: They're getting closer, I can hear them.

ME: I know, me too, let's hide in those trees (we run over to the floor lamp in my office. Alma looks up at me and I put my finger to my mouth) Sshh (I whisper, as Alma nods and we stand perfectly still for a minute. Alma makes an exaggerated gesture to show that she's not moving at all as she stands silently, almost holding her breath. Then, I wave with my hand for her to peek out of the trees with me.) I think they missed us.

ALMA: They could be back or close by.

ME: True, let's head this way but stay close to the trees in case we need to hide again. And let's be very, very quiet.

ALMA: Ok. Let's go. This way. I'll lead. (Alma starts to walk as I follow. We continue silently until she suddenly stops) I heard something!

For Alma, play was an opportunity to grapple with her prior attachment history and her fears. She had been controlling and her grown-up behavior belied a younger and vulnerable child who had already experienced the helplessness that comes when confronting fate. Born in a small village, raised first in an orphanage and then a foster home, Alma ultimately met a woman who would adopt her and become her mom. Dazzling on first impression, Alma grew bossier and moodier as she got to know people. As her play illustrates, she was also in a regular state of anxiety about how secure she could feel in her new home. I found that as Alma was able to use the play, not just to make up stories but to embody characters representing a range of feelings, such as anxiety, sadness, loss, and longing, she became calmer in our sessions and at home.

This was also the case with Sarah, who also created stories with trapped or missing characters who would pop in and out of the stories and transform themselves at any moment. Both children had been in a loop, repeating the same story in their play. In Alma's case, she re-enacted the same scenes when playing with her mother at home. Not surprisingly, her mom tired of this play and perhaps experienced some discomfort with Alma's focus on being kidnapped and taken by an evil witch. Alma's mother was certainly not such a person and was trying to create a loving and stimulating life for Alma in New York. But for Alma there was that fear that perhaps something could happen and she could be cast aside once more. When Alma first played out her stories with me, her play was relatively removed. Alma was happy to tell me about what was going to happen in the princess story and was even happier to direct me. But I wanted Alma to become an actor in the story. I wanted her to be able to embody the emotions that had come with her experiences. I wanted Alma to have the opportunity to tell her story, and her consequent fears, in a safe place with the emotional investment that would allow her to begin to move forward and develop her attachments and relationships.

As play with Alma continued, she began to branch out with her themes. The prince and princess gave way to other stories, characters, and expressive mediums, as Alma enjoyed my castle, action figures, paints and markers, and particularly, my fake food and kitchen utensils.

Food has played a role in understanding attachment since Harlow's early attachment research with rhesus monkeys (Harlow, 1958). Influenced by Bowlby's (1950) early theories of attachment emphasizing nurturance over biological sustenance as the most important factor in the relationship between a child and his or her primary caregiver, Harlow decided to test out some of these theories in research with primates. He set up two groups of baby rhesus monkeys and put them in two separate cages. In one cage was a '*mommy monkey*' who was made of wire but who had a feeding tube connected to her to provide milk. In the other cage was a '*mommy monkey*' made of wire but covered with a soft cloth material suited for cuddling. Harlow was interested in testing out how the baby monkeys developed and how they related to their respective '*mommies*'. He found that the baby monkeys from the cloth monkey became attached to the '*mommy monkey*,' and demonstrated improved health effects such as their ability to better digest the milk dispensed to them. So began much of the attachment research. Since then, a plethora of research has been devoted to exploring the relationship between children and parents with an eye on the importance of psychological attunement and secure attachment in a child's healthy development.

But, as anyone who's ever felt comforted with a warm bowl of soup or a refreshing bowl of ice cream can attest, food is a lot more than a bunch of mixed together ingredients, carrying with it a psychological meaning that will vary for each individual. It certainly did for Alma, who had quickly developed a sophisticated palate along with a near compulsive need to finish her food and try out the dishes of her fellow diners. Alma was always hungry. I wondered what this hunger was about as Alma ate as if she was worried that each meal might be her last for some time. An understandable stance for a child who had been through so many twists and turns in life. Not surprisingly, food started to make an appearance in our play as well, as Alma and I began to work on pretend recipes and kitchen organization.

ALMA: Let's take out the food. Do you have any kitchen things?

ME: Some. Take a look in that bin (I point to a blue bin in my toy closet).

ALMA: Hmm. (Alma rummages through the bin, finding some small plates, utensils, cups, a tea kettle, and an egg beater) Do you have any big plates? Any more pots? There isn't that much here.

ME: Well, look, here's a pot, some plates, forks and stuff, (I pick up another utensil) a teapot.

ALMA: (Sighs) We'll use that stuff. You should really get a kitchen. (Alma looks around the room, her eyes settling on a space near my bookcase) You could put it right over there. Then we could play with it.

ME: It's an idea. What kind of kitchen?

ALMA: You know, a kitchen.

ME: Yes, yes, but what should I have? I'm detecting a feeling that I may not have quite what I need here in the kitchen department so I'm just looking for some input here.

ALMA: You'd have more pots and pans, and an oven, and an area for cutting stuff. Also a sink. You could have lots of pretend food. Even more than you have.

ME: Sounds impressive.

ALMA: Oh, and it should be pink.

ME: Pink.

ALMA: Yeah, that would look really pretty. C'mon let's play.

ME: You want me to put a pink kitchen right over there, next to the nice rug.

ALMA: Uh huh. We have to make the food now. C'mon.

ME: What are we making?

ALMA: Lunch.

ME: What's for lunch?

ALMA: We're making it. (Alma starts to set up the tops of the bins as if they're trays and with my help starts to use a couple of empty bins as an oven and a sink. I help her put things in place, noting her creativity and resourcefulness in using these everyday items to arrange nearly the same kitchen she had just recommended.) I'm going to start cooking things. Let's see, let's make some pasta, some chicken, some vegetables, oh, there's some steak. (Alma notes the items as she begins to proceed through each and every food item in the bin. There are about 25 items in total and Alma goes through each one, occasionally pausing to express her satisfaction, with a smile and a lingering gaze, when she gets to a favorite item such as ice cream or a piece of pretend pink frosted chocolate cake. Finally, every piece of food is sitting, somewhat precariously yet neatly, atop a flat blue plastic tray.)

ME: Wow, that's a lot of food.

ALMA: (A satisfied look on her face) Everything is there!

I looked at the platter and my mind drifted again to a similar scenario with Sarah ten years earlier. I was in a different office with different toys. I also had pretend food, which Sarah would arrange carefully, and a large number of pretend animals, which she used to spend time arranging so that each animal was set up properly near its neighbor and no animals were ever left behind. Sarah had been particularly careful to make sure all the baby animals were placed right atop one of their parents, keeping the babies safe and preventing the baby and mommy/daddy animals from getting separated. Sarah had accounted for every animal and every food item, perhaps to avoid leaving anything behind. Once everyone was lined up properly, the animals could partake of the food or go on adventures, but always together. Over time, Sarah had allowed the animals to separate from one another for periods of time. As the animals grew more adventurous, Sarah's anxiety and hypervigilance had cooled as well. Interestingly, as she became less anxious, she was better able to rely on her parents to take care of any issues at home with her brother or at school, while Sarah allowed herself to act more like a child. As I remembered the array of the animals and the food, laid out so carefully, another voice was calling out to me.

ALMA: Hello, are you listening?

ME: Yes, sorry, my mind wandered for a second there.

ALMA: That was funny. I daydream sometimes too. Ok, let's make some food. Let's see, for breakfast we can eat (Alma looks over the food and starts picking items. As she does this, I start to associate to what she may have been eating back in her country before the adoption. I wonder about this association – is it my own projection or is it connected to our play?) We'll have some eggs, and some peaches… (Alma is listing food again. As she does so, I'm still wondering about this girl who has only been in New York City for about a year and who's completely focused on arranging a meal that looks like the breakfast buffet at the Courtyard Marriott.)

ME: What did you used to eat in India?

The question of when to stay in and when to step out of play is one of the most perplexing ones for any therapist. Staying in play allows for the richness and fullness of a metaphor to take hold, uninterrupted by a therapist's need to make the metaphor linear. Linearity is comforting for adults and can make a therapist feel that s/he is being 'therapeutic' but such linearity may not honor how a child comes to understand or manage his or world (Blake, 2011; Engel, 2006; Kronengold, 2010). On the other hand, there are times when stepping out of a metaphor can deepen a child's capacity to reflect on experience and to allow the metaphor to take on a fuller shape (Carnochan, 2010). It would be wonderful to have a clear decision-making tree for when to wonder about a child's metaphor and when to follow it. But, such decisions are generally in the province of clinical judgment that may wax and wane with any given child.

Alma was ridiculously verbal and comfortable expressing herself. She just didn't use words to express her feelings. With Alma I wanted to help her reconnect to a developmentally appropriate place by using her capacity for fantasy and play but I also realized that staying completely in play could in fact negate an important part of Alma. So, I decided to ask my question and with it, perhaps open another world for us to explore. "*What did you used to eat in India?*"

ALMA: What do you mean?

ME: Well, what did you used to eat? Back in India, it must have been different than this food.

ALMA: Oh, yeah. We didn't have all this. No hamburgers or hot dogs like in here. It's different there.

ME: I can imagine. (As we talk, we keep working on our pretend meal, arranging some food, putting dishes in our imaginary oven, and setting the table.)

ALMA: We ate dal bhat tarkari. (Alma says this very fast, as if swallowing the name of the dish in one gulp.)

ME: What is it?

ALMA: Dal bhat tarkari. (She repeats herself very fast, at least to my untrained ears.)

ME: Huh?

ALMA: (slightly annoyed) Dal bhat tarkari.

ME: (I still hadn't actually heard what Alma was saying very well. I give it my best knowing that I'm about to fail.) Dabat taka. Taka, taka?

ALMA: (laughing) No, no. Dal bhat tarkari.

ME: (I still don't know what she's saying so I say good naturedly) Could you slow this down a little? I'm having a hard time here. (As we slow down our pronunciation I notice that our work in the pretend kitchen is moving more slowly as well and Alma seems to be working on a dish unlike the ones I've seen her arrange before. She has a pretend fish in a bowl and only a couple of other ingredients near it.)

ALMA: Ok.

ME: Let's go piece by piece. What's the first part?

ALMA: Dal.

ME: Dal.

ALMA: Bhat.

ME: Bhat.

ALMA: Tarkari (she says this so it sounds more like tree).

ME: What? (as I scrunch my face and look at her hopefully).

ALMA: Ta-ka-ri.

ME: Ah! Ta-ka-ri. I've got it. Da, umm, wait (I'm trying to remember the first parts of the dish now but having a hard time). I can do this. Um, Da, ba, takari?

ALMA: (Rolls her eyes and laughs again) No silly. Dal bhat tarkari.

ME: You do realize I really can't keep up when you say that. Dhal, tak, tak, tak, umm. I don't know.

ALMA: I'm working on dinner now.

ME: Yeah, I'll help.

Alma and I kept on preparing dinner. I made some vegetables and it became clear to me that Alma was working on a particular dish rather than just using every ingredient in the office. As we talked about her home country and the food she used to eat, her relationship to the pretend food shifted. Alma has comfortably moved back and forth between play and talking, or better yet, imagination and reality. In fact, she appeared to integrate the two. Our conversation was followed by a shift in her menu, and then as Alma prepared the salmon, a dish with an added emotional resonance, our conversation shifted further. The humor between us allowed a playful quality to our back and forth and an added connection between Alma and me that allowed us to talk about a snippet of her life in India.

ME: Do you ever miss the food from your old home?

ALMA: Not really. I think about it sometimes. We have a lot of food here.

ME: Oh, ok. I was just wondering. You know like that dish, the (I'm still having trouble with the pronunciation. I feel at first a bit silly but then realize that there's an opportunity here, as my difficulty means Alma gets to be my guide to entering this part of her world) bhak something or other.

ALMA: (Laughs) Dal bhat tarkari. We thought of making it. But then we didn't. One day we will. Ok, this dinner is almost ready, I'm making salmon in a pot. There's salmon and I cook it in soy sauce.

ME: (I'm intrigued by how different this dish is from other pretend food creations.) Salmon and soy sauce.

ALMA: Yeah, we're making a salmon bowl. We need to make the soy sauce and we need some rice. Hmm. Do you have any soy sauce?

ME: No, but we can make some of our own.

ALMA: How?

ME: We can draw it.

ALMA: Good idea. (As Alma and I turn our attention to a drawing pad and art supplies, I start sketching little grains of rice while Alma draws the soy sauce. We spend a few minutes checking our designs and cutting out the pieces that we'll use for our dish.) Can you make some more of those, we need a lot of rice? Just drop them in the pot, it's already cooking (as Alma surveys the salmon pot).

ME: Sure. I'll make some more. (I take a whiff.) Smells good.

ALMA: Yup, it's going to be very delicious.

ME: I never made this sort of dish before.

ALMA: Really, oh, I make it all the time. You should try it, it's really good.

ME: I'm sure.

We worked on our salmon dish, with an almost meditative pace. Our play was quieter. We talked with each other but our exchanges, both verbally and nonverbally, were not as busy. There was a calm to Alma's play as for the first time it felt as if she had plenty of time and didn't need to rush as much information and content as possible in a session. It was hard to miss the connection between Alma's talking about her life back in India, the shift in how her food play moved from arranging items to creating something of her own, and her increasing calm in session. For Alma, and for Sarah and other children, our work was about finding a voice within the support of a therapeutic relationship. Alma could certainly hold her own, and is one of the more formidable four-year-olds I've ever met. But some of what seemed like a strong voice to others could be a smoke screen, her regular chatter and poise serving to obstruct a view of a child who had been through so many transitions and so much uncertainty. Alma needed to play out the dramas of the disappearing princess to connect with her earlier experiences. She needed to play out the making of the food, to reclaim a part of herself that would allow her to make a full transition in her new life in New York City with her adopted mother. In the same way, Sarah needed to bring me into her own family dramas and her desire to be found and never again lost.

Each of these children used play, in the context of a therapeutic relationship, to explore and understand elements of her past. Each child created vignettes that were strikingly similar in their depiction of missing princesses, forlorn princes and mothers, and ambiguously evil witches. Each child was unusually controlling in her play, working very hard to maintain direction over scenes that in an earlier time, had been far out of their control. Of course there were clear differences between the children, both in terms of the content of their play, their relationship to me, and their own personalities. But, their shared presentations and predilections speak loudly to their shared experiences and attachment histories. And their play speaks to a shared longing; a longing to understand, to connect, and to give voice to their experiences. It is precisely this longing that can be addressed and honored in giving these children an opportunity to engage and find their voice.

Permissions Acknowledgments

This chapter is adapted from the chapter "The Princess and Dal Bhat Tarkari: Play Therapy with Children of Cross-Cultural Adoption" of Malchiodi, C. A., & Crenshaw, D. A. (2013). *Creative arts and play therapy for attachment problems*. Reprinted with permission of Guilford Press.

7   Upside Down

"So, how's our chapter going?" a typically inquisitive David asked. I looked back skeptically, "Our chapter?" Pleased with himself, David continued, "Yes, how's it going? I want to make sure it's getting done," he smiled before adding, "I'm into this." I paused. "Ok, wait a second. Obviously I'm delighted with your enthusiasm. Now, if I may, I've been busy. Second of all, when did this become our chapter exactly?" David didn't miss a beat. "It's about me. Remember why you're writing about me in the first place. It's our chapter. We talked about this," and he sat back even more pleased. "Ok, ok, I get it," I continued, "I would just like to point out that I'm the one who's actually doing the writing. I understand that may be a minor point but I think it's worth mentioning." David laughed and continued. "So what are you going to call me. Make sure it's a good name." "Go ahead," I said wearily, "What do you want to be called?" "How about Marco?" I arched an eyebrow before repeating, "Marco." David looked at me expectedly, waiting for a response. "Why Marco?" I asked. "It sounds cool," David explained. "It sounds like you're from Milan?" I suggested. "Ok, how about Carlos?" I looked at David skeptically. "Jesus?" he offered. "I'm not feeling it," I gently noted. "Ok, just come up with a good name. It's important," David emphasized. "I'll do my best," I sighed.

So began a session with David, a name he found bland but suitable and which fit better than Carlos, Jesus, Maurice, Ivan, or the other potential candidates. After getting past my lateness writing this chapter, we returned to one of David's typical themes in our sessions. "Did I really have to come today? What's the point? You know how I feel," he protested. "It does seem to help you know," I answered for probably the hundredth time in the past six months. At this David's voice grew more animated. "I just want to make sure that you know. If you want to cancel, I'm really fine with it. I'm actually happy if that happens. You have no idea how happy I am. You know I hate coming here. I mean I hate it. It's my mother's thing I have to come. I hate therapy. I always have. It's useless!" I'd heard these words so many times over the past months I'd almost started to worry in the odd session David didn't remind me how much he hated therapy and how useless it was to him. It started to feel like some sort of disclaimer he needed to throw out each time he saw me. I responded with a tilt of my head upward as I feigned imagining assistance from above, "here we go," I said. "Yes, exactly. I just hate it here. I've never been helped by any therapist. I think the whole thing is idiotic! You have no idea how miserable I am in therapy. I hate it! There's no other word!" David's voice softened now, "By the way, I just want you to know I don't mean it personally." I let out a small smile, "thanks for the reassurance." David quieted down. I piped back up, "Any more on this or can we move ahead now?" "I'm good," David responded. "Sure? I don't want to get in the way of your expressiveness." "No, I'm solid. Thanks." Great," I replied and we started to talk about high school exams and David's fears.

Anxiety dominated David's life. He was fearful of crowded places, school trips, of an airplane crashing. He was fearful of going away to college, of sleeping outside of his house, of having a friend sleep in his own home. David's anxiety prevented him from getting close to other people. His state of upset, a terrible mix of simmering fears on the best of days, and waves of panic attacks on the worst, permeated David's life to the point that his daily routines and activities centered around trying to avoid these intolerable feelings.

When David was first referred to me, I was ambivalent about working with him. His fears had significantly disrupted his life. The result was a young man who greatly struggled because of his anxiety, despite his intelligence, natural warmth, and social aptitude. Prior to the start of his symptoms five years ago, David had enjoyed success in all areas of his developing life. My feeling was that David would best be served by a cognitive-behavioral approach that would focus on alleviating his symptoms of anxiety, and would help David with the thoughts, feelings, and concomitant physiological reactions to his fears. Such a symptom-based approach has to my mind proven its effectiveness in working with anxiety disorders. While I integrate such approaches in my work, I don't consider myself a cognitive-behavioral specialist and typically feel that a child or teen with significant anxiety symptoms such as David's will benefit from working with someone who is far more specialized and experienced in tailoring such a therapy. I explained my thinking to David's family, who appreciated my honesty, before listing the various cognitive-behavioral therapies that David had already tried, with little success. Each time, the work hadn't proceeded quickly enough and David had grown frustrated and dismissive of his prospects for change. The thinking, supported by the psychologist at David's school, was that my eclecticism, along with my playful style of working, might connect with David in a way that would support him through the ups and downs of our work. I told David's parents that I was willing to try. I would weave anxiety-specific discussions and strategies alongside my own preference for an open and casual therapeutic space, one in which David could breathe a bit, and that we'd assess how he was doing to see if our work was effective.

So, David and I met. He was a friendly and warm fifteen-year-old who easily took a seat in my office with a restlessness and a not altogether unappealing mix of stubborn anxiety and chronic curiosity. David began by complaining about his previous therapists. I noted to myself that his feelings about our initial appointment were likely similar. There was an older psychiatrist (David mentioned her age constantly) who had unnerved David with her stories about therapy. I wondered aloud how these stories had come about in their relationship but David was on a roll at this point detailing her faults. There was the therapist who scared David after talking about his experiences with severe psychiatric difficulties. There was the therapist who gave David homework. David didn't like homework generally and therapy homework even less. He went on ticking off names and therapies. David actually sounded impressive, with a lengthy therapy resume and a command of different therapeutic approaches. He was also very engaging throughout. Not in a way that suggested he was trying to appeal to me by criticizing other therapists, but in a genuinely warm manner. "So," I asked, "How are you feeling about our working together then? I mean, you've tried therapy a bunch of times." At this, David's smile receded. "Therapy won't help and I'll just feel worse. I know that. There's no reason for me to come here. This is a complete waste of time and money. My parents want me to come. That's it. What's the point of talking about my feelings? I'm just going to feel worse." David's words surprised, so coolly distant from the warmth of the rest of our session.

I always ask people, particularly after I've been asking multiple questions in an initial session or consultation, if they have any questions for me. As long as I'm comfortable with the questions, I'm happy to respect a child's or teen's appropriate interest that may be related to our working together. David didn't need the encouragement as the questions rained down. "How long have you been doing this?" "How many people have you seen?" "Where are you from?" "Where did you go to school?" "How long have you been in this office?" "Do you like what you do?" "Do you have kids?" "How old are they?" "What's your approach in therapy?" "Do you actually think it works?" "Have you ever helped anyone?" "Do you ever admit that you can't help someone?" "How many people have killed themselves while they were working with you?" "How old are the kids who come here?" "What do you do with the young ones?" "What's your favorite age to work with?" "Do you live around here?"

I didn't see this socially adept young man's questions as stemming from an unawareness of boundaries. Could they be a test in some way? Did he want to see how far he could push me with personal questions? But to what end? There are some teens who want to see whether I will set limits and ask me questions in order to see how much they can get away with in therapy, much in the way they gauge how much they can get away with with their parents. Maybe I was wrong but I didn't sense that David was the type to push limits. But what did he want with all these questions? I didn't get the uncomfortable feeling of someone who is trying to find out personal details as an intrusion. His questions felt pressured yet playful. Maybe they were deflections, attempts to change the topic of our sessions. After all, David was very clear how he felt about therapy and how little he felt it had helped him in the past. So, David was using the questions as a defense. But maybe there was more to it than that. What if David's questions weren't just a defense to change the topic as much as they protected him from the pain of another failed therapeutic experience while also engaging me from a safe distance? I wondered how David had felt the first time he tried therapy. Was he reluctant? Enthusiastic? Hopeful? Did he ask a dozen personal questions a session? What had happened to him over the years, as an initial bout of anxiety took hold, worsened and developed into a cycle of panic attacks that proved chronic and debilitating?

As I thought about David's difficult road over the past five years, I started to reconsider his questions. Many of us can struggle with anxiety but how does it feel to be so scared that you can't sleep away from your home or prepare your schoolwork? Imagine a very stressful moment in one's life and then imagine experiencing it all the time. The very image evokes such pain and sadness. Imagine how overwhelmed and out of control one must feel on a regular basis, as everyday worries turn into terrifying fears. Then imagine the idea that you have gone to see a professional to help rid you of this pain but the attempt to help, even if well-planned and executed, still fails. Then repeat that attempt several times, and try to imagine the feelings in going to see yet another professional. So, what if David needed to exert some control over his life in the very sessions designed to help him overcome his fears? What if David's questions were similar to a younger child's controlling play at the outset of therapy? What if David needed to be in the role of the therapist sometimes, the role to which we ascribe greater authority, asking me questions instead of answering them?

There's a long tradition of wondering about the place of self-disclosure in therapy. Figures such as Ferenczi (1949), Yalom (2002), and Beck (1990) represent psychoanalytic, humanistic, and cognitive-behavioral traditions that advocate for a measure of self-disclosure in therapy. But it's complicated. Self-disclosure has been written about extensively but often in relation to occasional queries. As I considered the start of my work with David, I wasn't familiar with anyone essentially trading questions with a child. In the humanistic tradition, Yalom has probably asked the most probing and provocative questions about the therapist's self-disclosure. That said, it is worth noting that his most provocative depiction occurred in his book *When Nietzsche Wept* (1993), where Yalom imagined a therapy between Joseph Breuer and Friedrich Nietzsche, where the esteemed Dr. Breuer and highly conflicted Nietzsche helped each other in equal turns. In some way this book reflects Yalom's belief of therapy as a journey of two fellow travelers. It may be important to mention that Yalom's book is also a work of fiction. I chose to answer David's questions, but I felt uncomfortable.

"Well, I've been doing this for a while now. I started my practice in 2000," I told David. "I can't say exactly how many people I've seen. I don't really keep count or anything. I'm from New York. I live around the neighborhood. I do enjoy the work and can't exactly define my approach. I mean, it kind of depends on what you have in mind," I blurted out, my pressured responses highlighting my discomfort. I looked at David again for a moment as he sat looking a little surprised. "I'm happy to continue but I'm just curious," I said a little too jovially. "Do you always ask this many questions?" David stiffened and was quiet for a moment. He looked back at me. "Just wondering," he said, his voice low and with little emotion. My question about his questions pushed him back into himself, and I tried to recover. I imagined what this session might look like from David's eyes, talking to a stranger about his fears and wondering why on earth he should think this person would actually help him. As I did so I felt better about his queries. "Ok," I continued. "I'm ok with answering any questions you have. Really. I mean, I may decide to not answer something if I'm not comfortable with it, which I hope you can understand. I imagine you wouldn't answer every question either." David nodded affirmatively, his face still looking surprised, as I kept talking. "Good. I mean let's look at the situation we're in right now. I started with a few questions and instead of answering them you asked me a whole bunch more. So, yeah, it makes sense I won't answer everything and," "Hold it, stop, wait," David interrupted, with a slight smile and an intense look in his eyes. "Are you always like this?" I looked up to the ceiling – "Always like what?" "Talking things out loud like this." "Sometimes." "Sometimes, when?" "Sometimes, sometimes." "What does that even mean?" "What if I told you I don't know." "I can live with that," David shrugged, as he relaxed sitting on my couch. Our absurdist exchange comforted David as it did me.

As I thought about our first session, and David's fast paced questions, I thought also of the faster pace of his worries. I wondered how to slow things down a little for him at the same time that I realized that I would need to meet David at a point of relative comfort for him. He enjoyed our banter and had a terrific sense of humor. I expected both would prove critical in our work and help me find a way to connect with David so that he might be able to start managing his heightened level of distress.

"Ok Doc, I came back," David looked at me as he sat down at his next session. "Indeed, delighted to see you again," I replied. "How was your week?" David asked. "Funny, I was about to ask you the same thing," I answered. David didn't respond and continued with his questions. "So, what did you do this weekend?" I looked at David with an "are we going to do this every week" look on my face. David continued, "Well, go ahead, how's your family by the way?" I thought for a second and decided to continue. I had in mind where I wanted to go but decided that with David, I would take a longer route. "They're ok, thanks for asking," I answered. David looked at me for a second with a hint of expectation in his eyes. He wanted more from me. "It wasn't anything particularly exciting. I went to the park, did some family stuff, helped with a little homework, cleaned up a bit." David wasn't thrilled. He asked me further, "What do you usually do on the weekend? Go to the park and do what?" I had no idea what he was getting at or wanted to know. I had started down this road of answering his many questions and wondered if I had made a mistake and would spend the next forty-five minutes recounting my grocery shopping on Sunday afternoon. "It depends. I mean there are my kids' soccer games so those take up some of the weekend." David was interested now and interrupted me. "Where do they play? School? Team? West Side Soccer?" So, now my kids were in the conversation. "They play on a travel team," I mentioned, as I referenced a team that has games in different parts of the city and suburbs. "So you have the games on the weekend. Then there's other stuff to do." "How much time do they put into travel?" David wondered. "Well, there's a game on the weekends and then there's practice which is two or three times a week." David arched his eyebrows for a second, "Impressive. Are they good?" I paused a second more. What on earth was I getting from this conversation? I could see the point if I was seeing David for therapy. That is, for myself. But he was seeing me and now I was supposed to give him information on my own kids' relative soccer talents. "Well, they're decent players." "Who's better?" "What do you mean who's better. I can't answer that one. I'm their dad!" David considered my response. "Ok, I see your point. That's ok. But are they really good or just good. Like can they play in college? Get a scholarship?" I made a questioning face as I answered, "Look I'm not an expert but to be honest I don't see it. They're solid New York City soccer players on decent travel teams. No one's turning pro or anything. They enjoy the game and it's kind of a family thing."

To my surprise, the conversation turned. "I play out there in Riverside Park sometimes," David offered, mentioning the park in our shared neighborhood. "Pickup games?" I asked. "Yeah," he said, "I was playing last week with these guys. One of them was seriously good. Like, I mean amazing. I think that kid could play anywhere. Like pro." "What could he do?" I wondered, "I mean what kinds of skills are we talking about?" "Incredible," David responded. "This guy was fast, strong, had moves. He was fantastic. I mean I go out there and I play and I'm ok but this guy was the best I've seen on the field. He could get a scholarship I'm sure. What do those guys make anyway?" "You mean in the pros?" I wondered. "Yes." "I don't think they make much here in the states. If they make it to Europe there's some money but it's a tough road. So, you're a soccer guy?" I asked. "I play for fun but basketball is my thing," David answered. What a novel idea.

"Where do you play?" I asked. "I play in a league with a travel team," David answered. "Where are the games?" I wondered, noting in my mind that the usually fearful David managed to handle the stress and travel of these games. "Different places, sometimes in the city, sometimes Westchester." "So, are you good?" "Decent. I have these games where I'm playing really well. Last season I had this run of games where I was seriously good. I mean good. There was this one game …" and with that David began to tell me about his basketball exploits, and most importantly, did more talking than I. I noted how David's comfort seemed to flow from his asking me questions. And my answering them.

David greeted me with his usual friendly smile for our next session. I began to ask about his week but I'm not sure why I bothered. "So, how's it going with you. What do most people call you?" David wondered. "Usually, I go by Henry," I explained. "Sometimes people prefer to call me Dr. Kronengold and then there's the Dr. Henry group." "Dr. Henry?" David laughed, "What is that?" As I answered I pointed inward, "well, *that*, is actually *me*," I pointed to myself. David was amused. "Dr. Henry?" He looked at me as if I had dressed up like a purple dinosaur. I chose to respond playfully. "You look judgmental," I answered back. David insisted, "No, no, not at all. I want to hear. Please go ahead." I looked at him, holding back a smile for the first time in our work. "I can sense those things you know. It's part of my training." David looked back at me, forming his own smile now. "Ok, please, Dr. Henry, tell me about your name." "Well," I continued, "It's one of those things I think where someone doesn't want to call me by my first name because they feel it's more respectful, but then Dr. Kronengold feels too formal, so, hence, Dr. Henry. A lot of people call me that you know." David listened, thought about it for a moment and continued. "It's cute." "Cute?" "Yes, cute. Dr. Henry. I like it. I'm going to call you Doc. Can I call you Doc?" "Sure, works for me," I concluded. "If you're happy, I'm happy." "Am I the only one to call you Doc?" "Well," as I drew out the word, thinking for a moment, "Not really, there have been a few people," as I noticed a disappointed David looking back at me. "Not many though," I said reassuringly. "Why? Is this a 'you want to be unique' thing?" David ignored this last comment and continued his questions. "So, Doc, have people changed what they call you over the years?" I was struck by David's perceptiveness. It so happens that he was right. As I've aged, more and more people have preferred to call me Doctor and fewer call me Henry. As we spoke I remembered the natural intuition of some of the most anxious kids that I've seen. There is something about the permeability of an anxious soul to the world around him or her that makes for such a stew of alternating vulnerability and insight. David was pleased but just for a moment as he abruptly shifted gears. "Have I mentioned I hate therapy?" David said. I was surprised and wondered about the sequence in our session. "Yes, one of the first things you told me." I knew David was growing more comfortable. Maybe he was getting too comfortable and needed to remind himself how little he thought of therapy so that he could regain some distance. It was very obvious to me that David liked our sessions, as did I, and that he wanted some help. As David went on with his protest I interrupted momentarily, "I have a question. First, I'm sorry for the interruption, I just need a minute and you can feel free to ignore me." I paused a second and then continued, "Why do you prefer talking about my life than yours?"

David looked at me silently for a moment, considering his response. I wasn't looking to take him off guard. On the contrary, I thought that was the worst thing to do. Catching him off guard meant eliciting his anxiety, which in turn led David to withdraw. It also meant betraying the closeness that we were building in our sessions. I needed to wait for the right moment when David and I were actually engaged in conversation, so that my question, though provocative, didn't startle him. The idea wasn't to show David I had discovered something about him nor was it to ambush David and prove how smart I was. Both are pitfalls in the work. Rather, I wanted to wait for the right time to ask David about his avoidance in a way that felt organic to our back and forth conversations and reflected my actual curiosity rather than judgment. He looked at me for another moment, and sat up a little in his chair, his body stiffening ever slightly. "I don't know." Then he shifted gears again, his voice turning angrier. "What's the point of my talking to you anyway?" David half-asked and half-declared. "It may help," I said, as I leaned forward with a bit more intensity in my own voice. At this, a more agitated David stood and began to pace around the room. I kept quiet and waited a moment. My question had clearly triggered a reaction and I wanted to help David through it while also giving him room for his feelings. "It never has. I've tried therapy before. I've tried it a lot of times," David's body was tense and his tone even angrier. "Therapy doesn't work for me. I'm telling you. It's a waste of time. Don't you see?" He paused a moment and I let him continue, though I wondered whether to break in. His eyes burning, David went on, "I hate it! Hate it! I've said that to you. I hate feeling this way! I hate talking about feeling this way!" David looked at me, his face an etching of searing upset. I wondered about reflecting his feelings but chose to engage David, as our relationship was based on this back and forth that we had started to develop. I felt the tension in my own body as I thought how to respond. I didn't want to say anything that came from my own anxiety nor did I want to leave David alone, as I could see the worry take hold of him. I breathed for a moment and then met David, my voice laced with its own intensity as I looked directly at him. "I see that you think it's stupid. I know it sucks to feel the way you do," I started, as David stared at me, taking in my words but looking distressed. "I know therapy hasn't helped you before," I paused. "I know you think you can't be helped," I paused again. "Ever." I took one more pause. "You have every right to feel that way. I just don't agree with you." I had spaced out what I wanted to say to give David a moment to take each piece in, and buy some time for him to calm himself. I hoped that each pause could give us a little space in which the intensity of David's feelings could prove digestible. "Ok, how? How is it going to help? Please tell me!" David paused again. He wasn't finished and I let him continue. "You don't understand what this feels like. I've tried before and nothing has worked. Nothing. Do you realize how lousy I feel? Do you understand? I used to be ok. I was normal. I went wherever I wanted. I did things. Now it sucks. I feel horrible all the time. I could barely get to school last year but the psychologist there, he helped me. He's the only one." David finally stopped, his body still coiled in a maze of emotions. I wanted to try to stay with this feeling, betting that if we could get through a moment of duress, that David would begin to tolerate other moments of discomfort in our sessions, be they between the two of us or about himself. "What did he do that helped?" I wondered, my voice landing from its earlier intensity. David continued to calm as well. "He'd talk to me. I was so nervous about getting to school, but he'd let me be in touch when I needed to," David explained. As he continued to speak, he grew more anxious again. "I still remember last year, when I finally got back to school, I was terrified getting there the first day and I called him. He met me, talked to me, calmed me down. He was good." "He actually helped," I noted, my voice rising a little to connect to David, who was starting to relax a little again. "He'd just talk to me. Mostly he'd listen and I'd talk and it helped me get through things." "Can I try to do the same?" I asked, tilting my head to the side. David responded, his hands moving now. "He was there though. He was at school. He'd be able to help me when I was having a panic attack. That's why he could help. What's the use here?" At this a pained expression came over David. "It's awful. Awful. Do you know what it feels like to have a panic attack?" I looked at David. "It feels like you're dying," I answered. "Yes, like I'm dying. Everything is messed up." As David put his head in his hands, I waited a moment before continuing. Steadying myself, I asked David, "What's going on right now?" "I hate feeling like this. I'm feeling miserable now just talking about it. That's why I don't like going to therapy." His voice grew louder. "I hate talking about this stuff! How are you supposed to help me?!"

With the tension in the room, answering was difficult. I felt anxious, and from that place, my comments would only spark David's upset. On the other hand, trying to be too calm would mean cutting myself off from my feelings and missing the emotion in the room, likely only worsening the situation. I gave myself a moment to both stay anxious and to soothe myself just enough to remember that I was in this room with a young man who was struggling. So I answered his latest question, or more aptly accusation, as honestly as I could. "How am I supposed to help you? It's a fair question. I kind of wonder the same thing actually." David stopped and looked back at me. The pause in between his question and my answer had given him a moment to collect himself as well. "What?" he looked in disbelief. I continued, "I wonder the same thing. Here's what I mean. I happen to think therapy helps. That's based on my own experience here. Now, I could be wrong of course and maybe I'm fooling myself." David looked surprised as I admitted to my doubts. "But," I continued, "I kind of always wonder about how therapy works." David smiled and looked a bit puzzled. "So you're not sure how what you do works." I hesitated for a moment before answering, "Yes." David couldn't resist this line of questioning now. "You come here every day! You see a lot of people, right? You've been doing this for years! Then why do you do it? And how can you charge money for this anyway if you don't know how this works?" I answered just as quickly. "Oh, because I think I can help people. That includes you by the way, just to go back to the earlier part of our conversation." David sat down again.

"But you have no idea why?" I motioned again with hands as if to say don't go too far. "Ok, maybe that's a bit of an exaggeration. It's not that I have no idea or anything. I actually have quite a few ideas. I'm just not sure if any of them are actually correct or what combination helps." David looked curious now, probably the most interested he'd been in anything I'd said in these first sessions together. "Keep going," he said. "Sure," as I collected my thoughts for a moment to decide how far along a theories and techniques of psychotherapy conversation I was going to go. "I could really discuss this for a while. It's kind of a thing of mine." David smiled at me now. "You think about this how often?" I scrunched my face doing a quick internal calculation. "Probably every other day." "While you're in a session?" "No, I have a professional responsibility." I looked at David with mock indignation. "You know that. I leave here at the end of the day and wonder what I did that day and why did it help. Any thoughts?" I turned to David. He looked surprised. "You're asking me?" "Sure," I explained, "you're an experienced therapy person." David moved in to finish the sentence. "Who thinks therapy is a waste of time." "Good point," I noted, "but you still have something to add. Was it ever helpful?" David answered quickly, "No. Not for a moment." I looked skeptically at him. "A moment?" "For real. Not a single moment was helpful." David looked determined now. "I hated every minute of it. Nothing helps, don't you get it?" His voice started to rise again and I wasn't interested in getting into a circular argument or upsetting him at this point. I was interested in his experience in therapy and how it related to our work together. I was starting to feel increasingly that David's ability to make headway with his anxiety would become rooted in his developing trust in our sessions. Whether that trust or the anxiety-reducing techniques we would start to discuss were most helpful was less of an interest and a question I would leave for my end of the day walk to the subway. "I don't want to argue. I get you think seeing me is nonsense." David calmed down and reassured me, "I told you it's not personal." I kept my voice calm but with an emotional tone to convey an appreciation of what David was telling me. "I know. I get that. I know it's not personal," gently swaying my head from side to side to convey my understanding. "What I don't get is why you're so completely convinced this is a waste of time."

I waited a moment. I knew David was still feeling upset but not as intensely as in the earlier part of our appointment. We had survived those earlier powerful moments and I decided to work further on David's anxiety as it came up in our session. "Can you tell me how you feel right now?" I asked David. "This moment?" he replied. "Yes," I said. David was silent for a moment. "I don't know." I paused again. "Try a little harder," I encouraged, regretting my choice of words. "Notice for a moment. It will feel a little weird but go with it. I know this is different." David responded quickly, "Even if I feel something, what's the point? I'll just feel bad!" I paused again. "I'm not guaranteeing anything. Just try," I nudged, as I thought about some other strategies that could work. David hated breathing exercises (he'd gone on about that in our first session together) so I'd hold on those. Maybe some self-talking or cognitive reframing of his feelings? My mind wandered as I quickly realized I was way ahead with strategies and my first move was going to be to help David realize what he was feeling. It seemed paradoxical, how a young man so intensely aware of his anxiety was in fact, not aware of his anxiety. That is, he wasn't seeing what was happening in his body as his worries began to worsen, a likely way of coping with the intensity of his feelings. David interrupted me, "I feel anxious." "Good. I mean I'm sorry to hear that but I'm glad you're noticing. How do you know?" I asked. "I just feel that way," answered David. "Ok, now notice your body." "It's kind of hard not to." "Yes, excellent point. So, notice your body. Do you feel the anxiety anywhere?" "What does that even mean?" "Just try it. Notice your body, the sensations you feel, and describe them. Start with your chest, what do you notice?" "I'm wearing a shirt," a smile crawled along David's face. "Inside your body. Your heartbeat, try that." "It's beating." "More good news. Describe it. Fast, slow, medium? Is it a typical heartbeat for you?" "I don't know. I don't usually monitor my heartbeat!" David noted, a slice of humor punctuating his observation. "Ah, the things you'll do and places you'll go. It will help. You'll see ..." And with that I talked to David about how anxiety gets registered in our bodies and gives us important signals as to how we may be feeling. Strategies to deal with it would come later. For now, I was thrilled to have the conversation, and to have taken things a step further in our sessions. I had David check in with himself and notice feelings in his chest, his head, his legs, anywhere in his body that would help alert him to burgeoning tension and potentially offer a way to relief as well. For David, it was his heartbeat, headaches, and stomach that held his anxiety.

"How are you feeling?" I asked David in our next session a couple of weeks later. "A little better." "Good. I'm glad to hear," I said before David quickly went on. "I still think coming here is a waste of time. I could be doing so many other things." I tried to answer reassuringly and with the humor that helped us stay connected. "Easy, easy, did I start some sort of therapy advertising campaign? Did I say, oh look how you felt better learning to stay with the anxiety? No, of course not. I mean I could have and now that you say it, maybe we should discuss the whole thing. I mean it is a decent point ..." David smiled at me as he was enjoying my rambling on. Finally, I concluded, "Never mind. Not looking to push my agenda or anything. I'm good. Enough about me."

For someone who hated therapy, David attended most of his sessions and was generally early. He was always very friendly and appeared happy to see me. He still had this need to ask me multiple questions about myself, my family, and my work. He wanted to know if I had vacation plans and favorite places to visit, how my kids were doing in school, where my wife and I liked to eat, etc. I want to be very clear. These questions and my report of them may be construed as intrusive, as there are some individuals who constantly test the boundaries of therapy in a manner that can be confusing to navigate for the therapist. As I hope is evident from the warmth of our exchanges, David was the farthest from such an individual that I had met. He was remarkably appealing, charming, warm, friendly, and ludicrously curious about the details of my life. It was this mix that led me to wonder about the place of his questions and the different roles that we may play in a therapy.

At a certain point I decided that David's questions had everything to do with his anxiety. It's too easy to dismiss them as defensive. Of course they were in part, and I had in fact alerted David to my thinking when I asked him if his questions were a way to deflect his upset feelings. But, more than that, his questions were a way to manage an otherwise overwhelming experience and I think, to connect to me. What if I respected David's needs? My experience thus far in our work had been that when I'd meet him at a place that he needed, that David would then take a chance in the therapy.

I admit that this decision was difficult. I don't have a problem with a degree of self-disclosure, particularly in working with children and adolescents for whom some knowledge about the person they're talking to is often important. Rather, it was the sheer volume and intensity that was different in my work with David. I hadn't worked with anyone who could easily have spent entire sessions, if left unchecked, asking me about my life. I also had to watch my own enjoyment in our sessions. I really liked working with David and our conversations were engaging, wide-ranging, and often great fun. There is a danger of having too much fun in a session. There is a danger for a therapist who is used to hearing about someone else's life to readily accept the invitation to talk about his own. This can be particularly true if that therapist, such as myself, likes to question some of the accepted orthodoxies of the therapeutic mainstream. It's very easy to say that a therapist should not, and cannot, be a wooden figure in the therapy room. But that's a straw man argument. It's in fact a lot easier to argue that a therapist needs to make sure that the therapy is based on the needs of the particular individual in his or her office and that the therapist needs to be careful not to get too easily swayed by a casual style that, under the guise of genuineness, can easily turn sloppy and unhelpful if not carefully monitored and questioned. The point is to make sure one is reflecting on disclosures, which admittedly may not always be so easy to do in fast-paced sessions such as David's. As questions bounced around my head, I took stock of David's progress in the past few months. He understood his anxiety better and was beginning to try certain cognitive techniques to help him reframe and challenge the depth of his anxious thoughts. As he connected to the reactions in his body, David became less reactive to them. The idea was not to banish the anxiety but to make it more bearable; to realize that a panic attack, however painful, would not kill him and would subside; to question if his conviction that he would never be able to leave his home was really true or a momentary feeling; and to see whether his belief that he was always feeling in a state of panic was accurate or an exaggeration. David's use of these strategies was crucial and his ability to use them clearly flowed from the connection that we made in his sessions. Our back and forth exchanges allowed David to feel supported so that he was not trying to solve his anxiety all on his own.

"Hey Doc," David said easily. While he slid comfortably onto the couch to begin his session, his wrinkled brow and pained expression suggested otherwise. "How's it going?" I asked. "No offense but you look a bit, something." David shook his head in agony. "It's awful. Awful. I can't do anything. I'm supposed to go on this school overnight trip and I don't think I can do it. I have finals coming up. It's too much stress. I'm not going to be able to go to college. I can't do anything. I'm always going to be like this! Do you understand that? Anything. I'm not normal!" David paused a moment before resuming. "I'm never going to be normal." He paused again, before asking, casually and honestly, "How was your weekend?" I looked at David quizzically. "You're serious?" I asked. "What?" David responded. "You tell me," I continued, "in the strongest way, how awful you feel. How you feel you're not normal, can't and won't be able to do anything, and then you ask about my weekend? Really? You know I'm not going to just let that one slide by." David shot back at me, "You don't think I'm normal?" "You said you're not normal," I countered. "As it so happens, I think you're very normal actually. You do suffer from significant anxiety and if I daresay, kind of an attitude about therapy, but normal? Not the problem." David listened and reassured me, "I told you it's not personal." "I know I know," I said as I waved my hand. "Please, tell me about how you're feeling," I implored. But David was resolute, "I'd rather hear about your weekend." "Really?" "Really." "Why?" I asked. "Because there's no point," David continued. "We discussed this already. I told you that therapy won't help me. All it does is make me feel worse. I feel terrible already." "Fine, fine," I relented, "we'll do it your way. My weekend was pretty average." "Yeah," as David motioned for me to continue. "It was nice out so I was in the park on Saturday." "Doing what?" he asked. "Took a stroll and played some soccer with my kids." "I was out there too," David interrupted. "I played some soccer and then some basketball. I was good," as David detailed his weekend basketball highlights. As he talked, and both discussed his weekend and asked me more about mine, David continued to relax. After a few minutes he shifted the conversation. "So listen, I have a question for you," David leaned as he prepared to ask away. "Go ahead," I said. "Why don't you play?" David asked me. "What do you mean why don't I play?" I looked back, a bit puzzled. "For real, in a league." Now I was even more puzzled. "Well, I kind of suck and I'm also pretty old at this point, though I do appreciate the vote of confidence." David waved his hands as if batting away my answers. "Excuses. You don't have to be any good at it. I think you should join a league. A chill one, just to enjoy the game. It will be good for you. That way when your kids get older you'll have people to play with. You see?" "See what?" I wondered. And a most satisfied David smiled back at me, "You're avoiding facing your fears. I'm looking out for you." "You've got to be kidding." "No, you know I'm right. You're scared to do it." "How do you know?" I protested, as David looked straight back at me with a knowing look. "Never mind," I continued, "I forgot I'm dealing with an expert." "Thanks," he smiled again. At this point he was lounging on the couch looking quite relaxed. "So how was the rest of the weekend?" he asked me. "It was ok," I said. "Saturday night?" David continued with his questions. "Watched a movie," I answered and then, looking at David appearing quite calm, I decided to take advantage of a pause to go back to our original subject. "Can we talk about the overnight now?" At that David was able to talk about his worries. He described his fear of having a panic attack, particularly in public with all of his friends around him. Impressively, David considered how he was catastrophizing his fears, allowing his earlier experiences to fully dictate what he thought was going to happen, and made a plan about how to deal with a panic attack in case he had one. A week later his parents emailed me letting me know that David had to miss our session for a school event but that he had successfully gone on the school retreat and enjoyed himself despite his fears.

David was relieved to have had a successful school trip but arrived two weeks later ready with more questions for me. "Which sports did you play as a kid?" David asked. I thought for a moment and responded, "The usual, basketball, baseball, football, some floor hockey. I'd love to talk about the trip, which I heard went well. Any chance?" "Yeah, yeah, later. Were you any good?" David wondered. "Not especially," I answered. "Ok," he settled into his seat, "What was your worst experience in a game?" I looked skeptically, "Why is this relevant?" David looked back just as skeptically, "We're supposed to be sharing. I feel better that way. So, worst experience," he motioned impatiently. "That one's easy, actually," I answered. David looked very interested now as he settled in and waved his hand for more detail. "Summer intercamp baseball game. It was a warm summer day in July of 1983, trees barely moving in the still summer air." "The story please," David interrupted. "Setting and context are important to the narrative. You should know that," I countered. David rolled his eyes and I continued, "So, I'm playing third base. That was my position. I was kind of a good arm but can't field third baseman. We're playing away at Camp Meadowlark. Their fans are all there having a good time. The batter comes up and hits a simple bouncer my way. Not a problem right?" David looks back expectantly. "Not exactly." I continued, "I make my first mistake. I should just charge the ball, throw the guy out and that's it. Instead, I decide to let it come to me because I trusted my arm, I mentioned I had a good arm, right? to throw the guy out." "You rushed the throw?" David wondered. "No, the ball took a funny hop because I didn't come in and bounced right over my head," I continued. "This doesn't sound so bad," David offered. I looked up to the ceiling in mock annoyance. "Can I tell the story?" David held his hands up as if asking for forgiveness, "Please." "Thank you," I added. "So, the ball goes over my head, I'm angry, maybe a little embarrassed at the moment, the fans are all enjoying themselves at my expense, and I go run to retrieve the ball from the edge of the infield. I grab it, and I see the runner is rounding first and is heading to second base. Remember, I had a good arm," as I nod to my right arm, David shaking his head to say, yes, I remember, I get it. "So in my head, I'm like, no way dude, I'm throwing you out at second." David nods affirmatively. "I wheel around, and fire the ball to second base to get the guy." David, leaning forward with interest asks, "Did you get him?" "So there was an issue." David looks at me with anticipation. "I didn't really set my feet, so I was pointing somewhere in between first and second base when I threw." "So where did it go?" "On a really nice direct path into right field." "Is that it?" he looked at me. I waved my hands in complete mock exasperation. "Fine. Go ahead, tell the story." David uses his hands to apologize again and adds, "I'm sorry, really. Please go ahead. I want to hear." "Are you sure? I mean, maybe you can tell it better?" "No, no. Please go ahead." I paused for a moment before continuing. "Ok, so now the guy is safe at second and to top it off, how's this for chutzpah, he decides to round second to go to third." I looked back at David who was intent on the end of my story now. "Well, my throw had been strong so it went right to the outfielder on one hop. He picks it up and makes a nice throw back to me over at third base to get the guy. I catch the ball, tag him, and pretend the whole thing never happened, right?" "I'm guessing wrong," David deadpanned. I sighed, "Sadly. Oh, so sadly, you guess correctly my friend. For a split second I take my eye off the ball to see where the runner is. Unfortunately, that's a bad idea as in that split second I lose track of the ball and only pick it up as it's coming in on me. It hits off my mitt and goes behind third base. The guy now starts rounding third. I get the ball and I have no chance, the entire camp of course has erupted in this miserable symphony of cheers and laughter. About a hundred kids are pointing at me and I've made three errors on one play and single handedly turned a ground ball out into an inside the park homer." "That's bad actually," David said, sounding impressed. "It was humiliating actually," I answered. "What did you do?" David wondered sympathetically. "What was I supposed to do. The next guy hit it straight at me and I threw him out. I threw it as hard as I could and almost took out our first baseman. I didn't talk to anyone for a couple of innings, I got over it, and here I am, telling you my story, though in rather excruciating detail considering it happened around thirty years ago. It's in the past. I'm good."

There's an energy you can notice in a session, much as you notice in any conversation. My three errors on one play story not only relaxed David but piqued his interest. Each step of the way he needed to know more about me and needed to see me as vulnerable and human. I noted to myself that we were moving in the direction of camp stories now, which were the beginning of David's panic attacks. I would love to say at this point David turned and started talking about all his anxieties, which in turn improved and together, David and I were able to do wonderful work, which had eluded his previous therapists. That didn't happen. At least not fully. David kept asking me questions. But, he also started to take more chances and worked on a gradual desensitization to his anxiety. Following the successful school trip, David started to go out more often, began to have people over at his house more and in a big step, spent more time at his friends' homes. He was beginning to confront his fears and in the process, lay down more benign and even positive experiences to slowly replace the older anxiety-ridden ones. These moments didn't all happen at once. They occurred over a slow and meandering course of several months.

As a therapist, it is easy to become comfortable in a particular role. Many of us find an approach that works and will continue to rely on that approach or stance regardless of the situations that we encounter, or more importantly, regardless of the person who walks into our office. It would have been easy for me to dismiss David and his questions. But sometimes, we need to take ourselves out of a comfort zone and take risks in order to help the individuals who come to therapy. I wasn't in David's head, so I can only speculate as to precisely what type of comfort he derived from his questions to me. The point is that he did, and if I hadn't taken this approach, I consider it unlikely I ever would have been able to help him.

But nothing is for free and I would soon learn that my comfort with the unconventional had its pitfalls. "Doc, I need to figure out what I'm doing for the summer," David brought up one session. I was delighted to hear him thinking about his next moves and asked, "What do you have in mind?" "I don't know," David shrugged before making a point of adding, "Don't bring up going away." I tipped my head sideways, "Really? You know I'm going ask you about that now. It's like a giant life size invitation that's begging me to please talk about your anxiety and to move forward into this next step, which would be both very exciting and brave by the way." David rushed in with a disclaimer, "Please don't think it's possible!" I sighed, "You're the one bringing it up and then getting angry at me about it." At this I changed my tone from casual to serious, as I wanted to examine this remaining fear more carefully. I dropped my voice a little, "You've thought about it." A clearly pained David looked down at the ground. "No, there's no way. It's how everything got started. I don't want to talk about it. Not now. I'm not ready." I wondered how far to push right now. I thought David was ready to talk about his fear but didn't want to overwhelm him. I also didn't want the fear to dictate his life or our sessions when I thought he was ready for more. "Ok, I get it. I'm not pushing it (pause) what if you're ready a little bit?" David shot right back at me, "You went to camp right?" So, we were back to the questions about me. I decided that if David needed a breather that was fine. Particularly as I hadn't exactly loved every camp experience I ever had and the conversation could be useful. "Yup." "Which ones?" "There were a few." "Did you like it?" "Sometimes," I explained. "I had my ups and downs overall. That's why there were a few." "Did you ever get homesick?" David wondered seriously. I had learned that sharing some of my anxiety happened to comfort David and while I wondered where we'd go and how far I'd reveal my summer camp history, I answered David. "Yes, I did." David was curious, his eyes locked on me, his body relaxed. "Did you call home?" he asked. "When I was upset?" I asked back. David nodded and I answered, "Yes." "They don't always let kids do that you know," he told me. "I remember. I had to push for it. Do you think it makes getting homesick worse?" he asked me. "It depends. By itself no. I think if a kid is calling all the time then it's a mistake. If you schedule it and keep it pretty short it can be helpful. It's not easy being away. In your case, I imagine they should have let you call." "Yeah," now David looked ahead wistfully, "I used to be amazing at camp. I was like the camp kid!" "I know," I said, remembering what David had described the one other time he talked about camp. David continued with his questions, getting closer to talking about himself while interspersing the ones about me as a break. Then he shifted gears again, "Do your kids go to camp?" I paused for a moment as I wasn't sure about talking about their camp experiences. But this had been our way in this therapy so I continued with David. "Yes," I answered. "Do they like it?" "My son does. My daughter at first liked it, then hated it, went to another camp, had to get through her bad experience, and now likes camp again." "So she went to a new one?" "Yes," I answered, hoping this could open up a conversation about new opportunities and experiences. I looked to turn the conversation back to David. "Want to tell me a bit about what happened?" David ignored me, "Which camp do they go to?"

Hundreds of overnight camps dot the Northeast region of the United States, as thousands of kids head out to experience a bit of the country and head for an independent experience away from home for at least part of the summer. In the next few moments of the session, I realized that I had picked the camp that David had attended several years earlier. The one he had first loved and where he had been an amazing all around camper, before suffering a series of painful and debilitating panic attacks that kick-started the past years of anxiety.

David's eyes widened and he took a moment to collect himself. "That camp played a big part of my life," he said softly as a sinking feeling set over me. "I loved it there. I was made for the place and I thought I'd keep going there every summer until I'd work there." He paused. I sat with David silently for a moment before I spoke. I waited for my own heartbeat to slow as I hadn't planned on this connection and was worried about how it would impact David and our work together. "I'm amazed to hear you talk about it that way considering what happened," I paused again, reminding myself that my own discomfort was important but I needed to focus on David. "I'm not pressuring, ok?" I paused again, watching my own heartbeat and breathing as I talked. "It may help to talk about what happened. I also realize of the hundreds of questions I've answered, this one may have been a mistake." David breathed in and out deeply and put his head in his hands again. I added, "It's up to you. I trust you'll tell me or not tell me based on what's best. It's your call. Forget about my connection to the place for a minute. Tell me if you want." I knew this last piece was so important to David, whose anxiety could feel so out of control. He needed to know that the story and feelings were his. I felt that David was ready to tell me about what happened at camp and that the telling would be therapeutic. We had been getting closer to this moment in our sessions. My disclosures had helped David feel comfortable but the impact of this last one was unexpected. While I had answered many questions in the therapy, the subject of our sessions was still David, with my experiences and self-disclosures serving as a way for him to measure and manage his own feelings. With this camp interconnection, I had intruded too much on our exploration and I needed to bring the session back to David. To do so, I needed to shift away from how I felt and move closer to David's feelings.

I waited another moment as David took a deep breath, steadied himself, and began. He had no more questions for me. Instead, he told me the story. How he had loved camp for several years and went back one summer as excited as always. How his anxiety had actually started a few months earlier and there had been a question as to whether he should really go to camp that year. How he had seen a therapist who was very certain in her approach and who had listened to his worries. She had strongly recommended that he attend camp that summer. So he did. He started out ok but then got sick and the panic attacks started. He couldn't sleep and couldn't function. Certain counselors had tried to help but others had hoped the problem would go away, or as can happen, became frustrated with David's struggles. He hadn't been able to call his parents who didn't realize what was happening to him. Two weeks later the camp called his parents to come pick him up. They took him home, still sick, exhausted, and weakened. I listened, as David told me the entire story, with great detail, opening a window into how he felt during those few weeks. As he ended he let out a deep breath. He had worked hard and told his story bravely. He ended with one more question for me. "Is your daughter ok?" "Yes," I answered softly, amazed as usual by David's empathy. Then I thanked him for asking about her and for telling me what had happened and how I understood why it had been so hard and why his anxiety was so overwhelming at times. It was time for us to stop.

I had prepared myself for David to come in tentatively to our next session. Instead, he greeted me warmly, sat down, and asked about my weekend as per our usual routine. There was a lighter feeling to his presence though. Something freer in the way he sat on my couch, relaxed and looked up at the ceiling and then at me. I asked him how he was feeling and if he had any reactions to our previous session. He assured me he was ok, he hadn't liked talking about his panic attacks but he understood why I wanted him to, and how I probably wouldn't be able to help him anyway. At least not much had changed, though David continued to progress. He started to do overnights and looked more intensely at programs for college and possible gap year programs abroad. His anxiety remained, but with less intensity as everyday challenges became less insurmountable. The idea had never been for David to become anxiety-free as much as it was for him to be able to put one foot in front of the other despite his nervous feelings.

I've often wondered how David's therapy might have progressed if I had taken a different approach. If I had ignored his questions, seen them as defenses, set limits on them. Would David have worked more easily on his anxiety? Would I have wasted less time or indulged myself less with our conversations? On the other hand, he had already tried therapy several times, was highly cynical about its effectiveness, and the depth of his anxiety suggested that a novel approach might be the answer.

But what of other children and teenagers who enter our offices. Adults have certain expectations about therapy. There's an etiquette, which means respecting the boundaries of therapy and the therapist's life. Adults of course wonder a great deal about their therapists' personal lives, but they are accustomed to the idea that those details will generally remain private and more an object of fantasy. Kids are typically under no such cultural pressure, particularly the more expressive ones. Kids in fact ask a lot of questions and most of us encourage children to maintain their curiosity and inquisitive natures. But does that mean that these questions need to be answered?

David enjoyed our particular brand of therapy. I don't think it was the disclosures themselves that were important as much as the connection and openness that David felt in our relationship. That is when he didn't claim to hate coming to our sessions. At some point he asked me what I do to relax. I told him I exercise a bit, read, go for a walk, and write. "What do you write about? Like novels?" I laughed, "No, I can't write like that. I write about therapy." "Do you ever get away from this stuff?" He laughed. "It's relaxing, ok? Kind of a creative outlet for me. I can't play an instrument and I can't paint. So, I write." "But what do you write?" "Therapy stories." "The ones that worked the best?" "Not really." "Your favorites?" David asked brightly. "No, not my favorites. I write about the people who made me think about therapy and what it is. The ones where something happened that might have been different and made me question the work in some way. So I write the story and it's my way of trying to figure things out." David's interest grew now, and as he leaned over it was clear where this was going. "So, are you going to write about me?" I smiled. "Funny you should mention it. I've been thinking about it. "David beamed, "Because I'm your favorite." I looked up, "No, not because you're my favorite. And yes, before you ask, I like working with you very much. But you make me think about therapy. We work differently than I typically do." "Because," and David paused, his hands flipping over, "I ask you all these questions!" I nodded affirmatively, "Yes, you do. And I answer them. And that's a big part of what we do in here, and I don't usually do that, so it makes me think about how things work in therapy." David was very pleased with himself, "I'm excited about this." "I can see. I'm glad you are actually." As we let a moment go by I wondered aloud, "Do you think we'll figure out the whole you asking me questions thing?" David shrugged, "Why shouldn't I?" That was certainly one way of looking at it. "What do you mean," I asked. David started, his voice rising a bit and I could see he would go on for a while. "How am I supposed to trust you if

I don't know anything about you? Think about it. I have anxiety and panic attacks. They've messed up my life. I've seen a bunch of therapists ..." and at that he was off and running, telling me about the stupidity of various ones. When he was done I returned to the first point he had made, which made me the most curious. "You said, 'How am I supposed to trust you if I don't know anything about you?'" David nodded, "Yeah, why would I? Why tell you stuff if I don't know if you can relate to anything I'm going through? So you can sit there and be all sure of yourself and say, 'do this,' or 'do that.' I need to know if you can relate to my life somehow. Also, that you're not so high and mighty either. So when you tell me about your life, I feel like I know something about you and can trust you. I need to have a personal connection. That's what's important. The connection. You need to write that." "Interesting," I said, "I agree with you about the connection but the answering questions part is complicated." "What do you mean?" David asked. "The whole overlapping camp experience thing," I said lightly. "Oh yeah, that was bad," David agreed. "See it's hard to know where to draw the line. It's that slippery slope thing," I noted. "Yeah, but we managed," David suggested. I paused for a second before I added, "If you had known about the camp connection earlier in therapy I suspect that would have been it." "You think?" David wondered. "I can't be sure, but it's pretty likely," I said. "We managed it because we knew each other pretty well already." "That could be," David agreed before he continued, "But I still needed you to answer all those questions." I looked at David again, nodding in agreement as I answered, "I know. I think you did. That's what makes the whole thing kind of interesting."

Why did I answer so many of David's questions? Was David the only teen who ever came into my office experiencing acute distress and desperately needing to feel a sense of control in his life? I don't think the answer can lie in his symptoms or in his particular age. While there needs to be a measure of openness in working with kids and teens, I still stay conservative regarding self-disclosure. Meaning that I need to feel there's a reason to disclose parts of my own life. I don't mean very basic questions like my favorite sports team, or how old I am, or whether I saw a particular movie. Those are basic conversation pieces that are typical for kids and teens and from which they will typically recoil if not answered honestly. The issue is of a more substantive and personal self-disclosure. The parts of my own life that may in some way intersect with a particular individual who is sitting across from me in my office. I don't think that such disclosures are inherently therapeutic and when misused can intrude upon a therapy. The therapist needs to ask him- or herself what the point of the disclosure is and what impact it will have on a child. Any therapist will enjoy working with particular individuals, as I enjoyed working with David, and there is a pull to be more revealing and more natural in the therapy. But that pull can lead to a blurring of boundaries and a relationship that while very real, may lose its therapeutic value. What is crucial is to remain reflective and aware of how such disclosures, not to mention the natural collisions that can occur between two people, are impacting the therapeutic space and relationship.

So why with David? Why work so unconventionally? What was the benefit of answering David's questions? How did my self-disclosure work together with a very conventional, and in fact, standardized form of anxiety exposure and cognitive behavioral therapeutic techniques to help David progress and feel less anxious in the world? I can talk about how David needed that degree of openness given his history. How David needed to learn to trust again in order for us to work together. How questions were part of his playfulness and a way for him to feel connected to me, his therapist. How our banter opened up a space in which he could begin to feel safe and explore his feelings and difficult experiences. These are all plausible ideas and I expect there are many others I may not have considered or remembered to write about. What I do know is that there are no simple answers. There are however, many complicated, engaging, sometimes provocative, occasionally frustrating, but hopefully always stimulating, questions.

References

Ainsworth, M., Blehar, M., Waters, E., & Wall, S. (1978). *Patterns of attachment: Psychological study of the strange situation*. Hillsdale: Erlbaum.

Altman, N. (1997). The case of Ronald: Oedipal issues in the treatment of a seven-year-old boy. *Psychoanalytic Dialogues, 7*, 725–739.

Axline, V. (1947). *Play therapy*. Boston: Houghton-Mifflin.

Barish, K. (2010). *Emotions in child psychotherapy*. New York: Oxford University Press.

Barrows, P. (2002). Becoming verbal: Autism, trauma and playfulness. *Journal of Child Psychotherapy, 28*, 53–72.

Beck, A., & Freeman, A. (1990). *Cognitive therapy of personality disorders*. New York: Harper & Row.

Bellinson, J. (2002). *Children's use of board games in psychotherapy*. New York: Jason Aronson.

Blake, P. (2011). *Child and adolescent psychotherapy*. London: Karnac.

Bonovitz, C. (2009). Countertransference in child psychoanalytic psychotherapy: The emergence of the analyst's childhood. *Psychoanalytic Psychology, 26*, 235–245.

Bowlby, J. (1950). *Maternal care and maternal health*. London: Jason Aronson.

Bowlby, J. (1973). *Attachment and loss: Volume II. Separation: Anxiety and anger*. New York: Basic Books.

Caldwell, C. (2003). Adult group play therapy: Passion and purpose. In C.E. Schaefer (Ed.), *Play therapy with adults*. New Jersey: John Wiley.

Carlberg, G. (1997). Laughter opens the door: Turning points in child psychotherapy. *Journal of Child Psychotherapy, 23*, 331–349.

Carnochan, P. (2010). Earning reality. *Journal of Infant Child and Adolescent Psychotherapy, 9*, 26–33.

Cattanach, A. (1997). *Children's stories in play therapy*. London: Jessica Kingsley.

Chethik, M. (2003). *Techniques of child therapy: Psychodynamic strategies*. 2nd ed. New York: Guilford Press.

Crenshaw, D. (2006). *Evocative strategies in child and adolescent psychotherapy*. New York: Jason Aronson.

Crenshaw, D. A., & Kenney-Noziska, S. (2014). Therapeutic presence in play therapy. *International Journal of Play Therapy, 23*, 31–43.

Engel, S. L. (2006). *Real kids: Creating meaning in everyday life*. Cambridge, MA: Harvard University Press.

Ferenczi, S. (1949). Confusion of the tongues between the adults and the child: The language of tenderness and passion. *International Journal of Psychoanalysis, 30*, 225–230.

Ferro, A. (1999). *The bi-personal field. Experiences in child analysis.* London: Routledge.

Frankel, J. (1998). The play's the thing: How essential processes of therapy are seen most clearly in child therapy. *Psychoanalytic Dialogues, 8,* 149–162.

Gallo-Lopez, L. (2005). Drama therapy with adolescents. In L. Gallo-Lopez & C. E. Schaefer (Eds.), *Play therapy with adolescents.* New York: Jason Aronson.

Harlow, H. (1958). The nature of love. *American Psychologist, 13,* 573–685.

Hornby, N. (2005). *Fever pitch.* London: Penguin.

Hudak, D. (2000). The therapeutic use of ball play in psychotherapy with children. *International Journal of Play Therapy, 9,* 1–10.

Jennings, S. (1990). *Dramatherapy with families, groups, and individuals.* London: Jessica Kingsley.

Jennings, S. (2011). *Healthy attachments and neurodramatic play.* London: Jessica Kingsley.

Kaduson, H. G. (2006). Release therapy for children with posttraumatic stress disorder. In H.G. Kaduson & C.E. Schaefer (Eds.), *Short-term play therapy for children,* 2nd ed. New York: Guilford Press.

Kleimberg, L. (1998). Playing and illusion in psychoanalysis and football. Paper given at the 'Football Passions' conference organized by the Freud Museum and University of East London.

Kronengold, H. (2010). Hey Toy Man. *Journal of Infant, Child and Adolescent Psychotherapy, 9,* 3–17.

Lanyado, M. (2004). *The presence of the therapist: Treating childhood trauma.* London: Routledge.

Loewald, H. W. (1960). On the therapeutic action of psychoanalysis. *International Journal of Psychoanalysis, 41,* 16–33.

Moustakas, C. (1997). *Relationship play therapy.* Lanham, MD: Jason Aronson.

Oaklander, V. (1988). *Windows to our children: A Gestalt therapy approach to children and adolescents.* Highland: The Gestalt Journal Press.

Schoop, T. (1974). *Won't you join the dance? A dancer's essay into the treatment of psychosis.* Palo Alto: National Press.

Stern, D., Sander, L., Nahum, J., Harrison, A., Lyons-Ruth, K., Morgan, A., Bruschweiler-Stern, N., & Tronick, E. (1998). Non-interpretive mechanisms in psychoanalytic therapy: The "something more" than interpretation. *International Journal of Psychoanalysis, 79,* 903–21.

Val Fleet, R. (2010). *Child-centered play therapy.* New York: Guilford Press.

Winnicott, D. W. (1965). *The maturational processes and the facilitating environment.* London: Hogarth.

Winnicott, D. W. (1971). *Playing and reality.* London: Tavistock.

Yalom, I. D. (1993). *When Nietzsche wept.* New York: Harper Perennial.

Yalom, I. D. (2002). *The gift of therapy: An open letter to a new generation of therapists and their patients.* New York: Harper Collins.

Index